ANTHROPOLOGICAL AND MEDICAL STVDIES ON
PEDERASTY IN EVROPE

BY
Prof. BENJAMIN TARNOWSKY

Fredonia Books
Amsterdam, The Nrtherlands

Anthropological, Legal and Medical Studies on Pederasty in Europe

by
Prof. Benjamin Tarnowsky

ISBN: 1-58963-323-7

Reprinted from the 1967 edition

Fredonia Books
Amsterdam, the Netherlands
http://www.fredoniabooks.com

CONTENTS
**Perversions of the Sexual Instinct—
Clinical and Medico-Legal Methods:
A Contrast**

Perversions of the sex instinct—Contrast between medico-legal and clinical methods—Depravity, inveterate vice or disease—Diaries and autobiographies of perverts—Classic treatises of Casper and of Tardieu—Specialists in disorders of sex—Frank confessions of perverts—Private admissions of pederasts —Offenses against public morality.

I. The Various Types of Pederasts

Varieties of pederasty—Greek love— Pederasty and other perversions—Psychopathic temperament—Innate pederasty—Acquired pederasty—Sexual depravities in age and disease—Differential diagnosis according to type of pederasty.

II. Voluptuous Strangeness of Pederasty

Perverted modes of sex—Boys' abnormal love for men—Signs of pederasty in childhood—Voluptuous strangeness of pederasty—Woman's seductive attitudes and the pederast—Pathological fleshly urge of pederasty—Coitus with women — Pederastic dreams — Feminine allurements of pederasts—How they attract men—A woman's soul in a man's body—Anthropological studies of Ulrich in homosexual love—Detailed confessions of a psychopath—Professor Mierzejewsky—Marriage of a pederast

—Queer sexual behavior of congenital pederasts—Taylor's important observation—Elisa Edwards, male "adventuress and actress"—Normally developed genitals—Numerous lovers—His amorous adventures with men—"Conaedus" Coquetry of catamites — Playing the woman's part—Sex tragedies from ignorance of teachers and parents—Prevention of maturing pederasty—Sexual erethism of the posterior—Flagellation, onanism and pederasty — Imperative need for erotic brutality—Normal performance of the sexual function.

III.   Curiosities of Pederastic Desire   **27**
Flogging as a cause of pederasty—Nocturnal pollutions—Dr. Albert's erotic accusation of teachers—Pederastic desire for old men—Born pederasts and greybeards—Fantastic erethism from inanimate objects—Case of fur amorousness—Charcot and Magnan *Inversion du sens génital*—Erotic hallucinations—Irregular development of genitals as sign—Stealing for sexual satisfaction —Dr. Krauss' and Dr. Eulenberg's reports—Spermatic emission from tearing—Lombroso's psychopathic example of perverted murderer.

**IV.   Sexual Crimes of
        European Perverts**   **35**
Monstrous forms of sexual satisfaction —Violation of little children—Lewd desire to rape and kill—Demme's two curious observations — Invincible sex urge to wound women—Erotic blood-

lust of Augsburg wine merchant—Powerful sexuality—Fifty attacks on pretty girls—Arrest—Case of Xaver of Botzen—Pleasure from inflicting genital wounds—European cases of erotic cannibalism — Execution of Menesclou in Paris—A crime of psychopathologists: Lasègue, Brouardel, Motet—Fatal discovery in anthropological laboratory.

V. Staggering Lust-Crimes of French —Sergeant Bertrand: Detailed Confessions   **41**

Staggering French affair of Sergeant Bertrand—Detailed description of his erotic crimes—Bertrand's shuddering revelations in his own words—Ravishing corpses—With dead animals—Demoniac enjoyment—Profanation of disinterred bodies—Mad pleasure of dismembering—French madman describes grotesque eroticism—His own explanation of his insane lust—Bertrand's further confessions to Marchal de Calvis —His erotic crimes at Douai and Béré —Predisposition to congenital pederasty—Sexual frenzies in cretinism—Bestiality of idiots—Drunkenness of parents at time of procreative act—Its terrible consequence—Pederasts born of syphilitic parents — Cases — Mountainous cradles of pederasty—Alps, Himalayas, Cordilleras — Persian affirmation: original cradle of pederasty—Effect of altitudes on sexual desire and potency —Acts of sodomy—Effect of education on predisposed pederasts—Sexual guid-

ance, society and pederasty—Shaw and
Ferris on perverted sexual instinct—
Curing born pederasts—Treatments of
Charcot and Magnan—Marriage, inter-
course of pederasts with women.

**VI. Celebrated Affairs and Trials
for Criminal Eroticism**   **53**

Normal men as periodic pederasts—
Periodic desire for abnormal sex act—
Active pederasty and flagellation—Married men as pederasts—Urge for coarse-
ness and indecency of normal men—
Elaborate sexual arrangements — A
queer case — Pederastic seduction of
boys — Secret seductions — Perversions
in a bathing establishment—Celebrated
trial of "Rue Basse des Remparts" in
Paris—French trial of 47 persons for
sodomy — Lasègue's periodic exhibitionists—Pederastic attacks and normal coitus—Precautions for maintaining secrecy—Outward signs of habitual
pederasty—Sudden unmasking of debauchees—Krafft-Ebing's case of periodic bestiality — Viennese engineer:
pathological violation of old woman—
Criminal sodomy on a child—Court decision—Van Gock's case of maniacal
erethism—Pederasty and suicide of famous French general—Léo Taxil's mys-
terious case in well-known Parisian
brothel—Brierre de Boismont's report
of necrophilistic rape—*Gazette Médicale*—Life imprisonment for violation
of corpses—Anjel's description of paroxysm of abnormal sex desire.

VII. Analyses of Legal Psychiatry in Russia   **69**

Pederasty and epilepsy—Common origin of epilepsy and sexual perversions —Mysticism, megalomania, sexual perversion—Case of pederastic rape and rape of girl—Followed by epileptic fits —Dr. Erlicki's case of public eroticism of brilliant epileptic—Dr. Kowalewski of Kharkov's communication—Analyses of Legal Psychiatry—Strange excesses of a Russian—Judicial investigation—French case of Legrand du Saulle.

VIII. Erotomania and Ecstatic Pederastomania   **77**

Erotomania—Erotomaniacs and abnormal coitus—Platonic love with prostitutes — Ecstatic pederastomania — Gorry's *fièvre érotique* — Pederastic acts with statues—Diaries and memoirs of catamites—Clysophus and his beloved statue—Greek pederasty with Cupid— Exceptional case in St. Petersburg—Dr. Raggi and sexual maniacs—Wine as stimulant to abnormal sex acts—Moreau de Tours and great magnification of sex desire—Amatory confession of Abbé de Cours—Visions of St. Anthony —Léger's execution for rape and murder—*Pocula amatoria*: aphrodisiacs— Acute Priapism.

IX. Pederasty Among Boys— Preventions   **87**

Pederasty in boarding schools—Morbid intensification—Pederasty and masculine women — Pedicator's impotence with women—Lowest depths of pederasty—Schools as centers of pederasty—"Venal passive pederast"—Degeneration of boys described—Depravity of prostituted pederasts—Wine and wild orgies—Promulgation centers of pederasty—Sailing vessels, prisons, army barracks—Health and sex intensity—Intensity, duration, frequency—Occasional pederasty as normal sex stimulant — Effeminate catamites — Pederastic excitation and impotence—A powerful agent for provoking pederasty—Parisian *stercoraries*—A revolting vice—Special arrangements in houses of prostitution—Marquis de Sade's plea for pederasty — Monomaniacal debauchee seeks ever new stimulants.

X.   **Pederasty in the Orient**   97
Pederasty in the Orient—Endemic state among several Oriental peoples—Oriental religions and pederasty—Moslem soil favorable for pederasty—Open display of pederasty among Oriental rich—Sexual abuse in Society—Powerful provocative — Mussulman maintains troups of young pederasts—Mistresses and beautiful boys—Intellectuality and pederasty in the Orient—Pederasty and Oriental law.

XI. **Pederasty in Old Men: Perils—
Horrors of Marshal Gilles de Rais**   101
Sexual perversions in old men—Age and deviation of sexual sense—Brain and skull decay and sex perversions—Senile dementia, indecency and pederas-

ty—Public outrages against decency by
old men—Lewd exhibitions in public—
"Renifleurs" — Astounding vices —
Tardieu's description—Senile bestiality—Cruel child-sexuality of old men—
Morbid desires kindled—Peril of sexual perversion in the aged—Schopenhauer on pederasty as a good—The
great evil it prevents—Psychopaths and
dissolute men—Case in Russian jurisprudence—Pederastic murder of 800
children!—Marshal Gilles de Rais of
France—Burnt alive for unequalled excesses and murder of children—His
haunting, horrifying confession—Inexplicable ecstasy in violation and murder.

**XII. Pederasts and Catamites—
Russian Cases**   **111**

Sexual perversion in idiocy—Pederasty and sexual debauchery—Model father begins to frequent prostitutes—Patient has recourse to pederasty—Fla-
grancy of paralytic pederasty—Paresis
of vaso-motor nerves—Effrontery of
his proposals — Practicing pederasty
with catamites—Report of Dr. Negris
—Sodomy, morbid sex desires in maniacs—Exacerbation of the procreative
sense — Priapism — A Russian picture
—A case at Academy of St. Petersburg
—Extravagant orgies—Athenian nights
—Loss of voluptuous sensation—Victims of venereal excesses—Pederasty,
sodomy, silver needles—*Tubes dorsalis.*

**XIII. Etiology of Sex Perversions—
Societies of Pederasts**   **119**

Etiology of sexual perversions—Variet-
ties and combinations—Pederast and
gratification of his abnormal leanings
—Societies of pederasts and catamites
—Morbidity and wild license—Terrifying indecency—Dual arrangements
and prostitution of pederasts—New variants of vice—Transformation into fel-
lators—Nervous system and congenital
pederasts—Refinements of gratification
—Tardieu's description of acts of fellator — Clubs — Pederasts and mannish
women—Physiognomic traits as sex
stimulants—Unnatural forms of union
—Amorous intrigues with boys and
women—Brutality in acts of pederasty
—Syphilis and pederasty.

**XIV.   Pederasty Among Roman Emperors
—Roman magnification of
Sexuality   127**

Sexual perversions of Roman Emperors—Rampant vices of the Caesars—
Boundless license on hereditary soil—
Epilepsy and exaggerated sex instincts
of Caesar—Refinements of depravity—
Vitellius' induction into vice—Role of
pisciculi—Vitellius became an habitual pederast—Public pederasty of Heliogabalus—Pederastic entry into Rome—
Women's clothes and had himself called
"Empress"—Castrated lovers in Oriental fashion—Inversion as a fellator—
Emperor Hadrian and passive pederasty—Description of psychopathic emper-
or by contemporary—Terrible depravity of Nero—Violating a vestal virgin
—Castration of Sporus—Passive ped-

erast to his slave—Wedded a eunuch
—Nero as wife—Suetonius—Petronius—Orgies—License ultra-refined by
science—All powerful Roman Emper-
or and Russian soldier—Roman magnification of sexuality.

**XV.   Antiquity of Pederasty—Pederastic
Blackmail—Russian Officials   133**
Antiquity of pederasty—India, China,
Japan, Persia, Greece—Origin and
spread of pederasty—Ratio of sex perversions to progress—Pederasty in Russia, France, England, Italy—Procurers
—Paris surveillance of male prostitution—Police and squad of pederasts—
Fees of catamites and prostitutes in St.
Petersburg—"Gentlemen's pleasures" in
Russia — Blackmail — Pederastic cases
in Russian courts—Rapid increase of
pederasty in Russia—Why?—Blackmail by Parisian pederasts—Catamite-
informers—Accusation of pederasty of
Russian official—Mercenary pederasts
"frame" officials—Some trials cited—
Pederastic racketeers—In bathing establishments—Legal investigations in
Russia—Audacity of Master-blackmailers.

XVI.   Sexual Problems of Law Courts   143
Errors of legal medicine—Confusion of
pederasty and sodomy—Legal cases of
sexual crime—Simian skull—Tardieu's
monograph on pederasty—His opinion
on unnatural acts of pederasty—Criminal punishment of psychopaths—Congenital pederasty, pederastic assaults

and punishment by law—Education and
treatment—A monstrous sexual crime,
and the law—Execution of insane per-
vert—Dr. Evrard's revolt—What type
of pederast should be punished by law
and which not—Sexual problems of
law courts.

**XVII. Physical Examinations
        for Pederasty   149**
Technical examination for pederasty—
Certainty in passive forms of pederasty
—Deformations in anal orifice—Sexual tests by medico-legal experts—Clinical examination more certain—Intimate diagnosis of 29 pederasts—Description of physical deformations of
habitual   catamites   —   Physiological
proofs—Digital exploration of rectum
—Infundibuliform anus of catamites—
Positions—Professor Brouardel's methods — Tardiue's — Tarnowsky's — Similarity of pederastic anus to assaulted
genitalia of little girls—*Podice Laevi,*
classic sign of sodomy—Flesh gluteal
region of normal men—Rectal intromission of sex organ—Signs of—Med-
ico-legists   and   passive   pederasty—
Symptoms of pederasty according to age
—Gaping of anal orifice—Exploration
of anus—Positions of old catamites—
Fissures and passive pederasty—Disgust and repulsion of odors.

**XVIII. Modes of Contamination
         of Pederasts   165**
Syphilis and sodomy—Various modes
of   contamination—Genitalia   through

coitus—Mouth through kissing—Syphilis in acquired catamites and pederasts —Fabrications of mercenary catamites —Young catamites at Imperial Academy in Russia—Chancres on genitalia —Observations on women at Kalinkin hospital — Sodomy among Russian women and prostitutes—Gonorrhea in sodomists — Onanism and sodomy — Papillomas as signs of sodomy—Cavity of habitual passive pederasts—Dispute between Casper and Tarnowsky.

XIX.   **Cases of Sodomistic Rape—Causes**   **175**
Sodomistic rape by impulsive pederasts — Preliminary training — Revealing signs of sodomistic rape—Extreme violence of assaults—Frightful case reported by Tardieu—Barbarity of sodomistic violation of children—Erotic cannibalism of attacks—Dr. Marquisi's descriptions—Dr. Espallac's case of sodomy on a girl of twelve—Tardieu's report on the penes of 133 active pederasts—Sexual parts of degenerates—Etiology of sexual abnormality.

XX.   **Establishing Nature of Inversion**   **183**
Forms of pederasty; sodomy, fellation —Establishing the nature of sexual inversion—Determining the responsibility of the pederast—Pederasts and coition with women—Voluntary and premeditated depravation.

XXI.   **Age, Pederasty, Punishments**   **187**
Pederasty and dying sex potency—Sexual excesses and intellectual decay—

Increased lust and criminal acts—Age
and insatiability of desire—Depraved
individual seeks new procedure for intensifying erethism—Reading of pornographic works—External and internal sex stimulates—Incessantly growing
sexual erethism—Where vice ends and
disease begins—Contrast between erotic
acts of depraved man and diseased per-
vert—Hotbloodedness vs. depravity—
How to treat medico-legal cases of perversion.

XXII. Sexual Physiology in Jurisprudence   195
Gradual sexual corruption of a child—
Vicious education—Rape by force—
Which is more to be punished?—Maudsley's border zone between crime and insanity—Scientific basis for distinction
—Epicureanism vs. vice—Completer
ways of satisfying sexual instinct—Jurisprudence as a medical science based
on physiology—Solution by combined
efforts of physicians, jurists, sociologists
and philosophers.

**Bibliography of Important Works Treating
with Sexual Inversion and Pederasty   201**

Perversions of the Sexual Instinct

A Contrast Between Clinical and Medico-legal Methods

Five years ago I was called upon in the capacity of expert to give my opinion in a case of pederasty. While reviewing the data that I had collected on the subject, and comparing them with corresponding portions of the most widely circulated manuals of legal medicine, I was struck by the disagreement which exists between the assertions of official science, on the one hand, and clinical facts, on the other.

Each new technical examination revealed to me with greater clarity both the insufficiency of knowledge contained in handbooks having reference to perversion of the sexual instinct, and the inexactness of many of the principles indicated to guide objective examination in cases of this kind.

The subsequent studies made in this class of ideas by Krafft-Ebing, Lombroso, Charcot, Magnan and other alienists have made it impossible from now on to accept the old opinions, and they have strengthened my conviction as to the accuracy of the conclusions I have drawn from clinical observation.

The difference of opinion which obtained between the medico-legal expert and the clinician has at the present time become so considerable, that in order to explain these discrepancies, the absolute need arises for indicating the grounds of support for furnishing fairly correct answers to the questions posed by legal medicine, and to prepare the way for a wider, more uniform, and more fruitful study of the subject.

The medico-legal expert sees depravity, satiation of desire, inveterate vice and perversity where the clinician recognizes with certainty the symptoms of a morbid state with its typical evolution and conclusion. Where the first would strike at vice, the second prepares a brief to demonstrate the necessity for a rational therapy. On the other hand, there is a whole series of acts which the law punishes relatively lightly, in which the medico-legal expert sees only impropriety, caprice, or amusement pushed too far, and where he is always cognizant of the moral responsibility of the culprit, whereas the clinician discerns the inception of a serious malady, the initial stage of an incurable psychic disorder, for which exacting attention and treatment are indispensable. Lastly, the clinician discloses real depravement, complete moral collapse, where the medico-legal expert is more often inclined to look upon the wrong-doer as the victim of fraud and violence.

It is certainly not difficult to understand why the observations and conclusions of the clinician must prevail, when our concern is the discovery of the truth in cases of perversion of sexual activity. The medico-legal expert deals exclusively with prisoners at the bar, who seek above all to escape punishment, and because of this, will most of the time deny obvious facts. Even in the rare case where he frankly admits his guilt, the accused has no reason to describe the intimate causes and motives for his acts. The physician testifying appears to him to be naturally an accuser rather than a defender, and when, resigned to the impending sentence, he confesses his deeds, he has nothing to gain by making this danger-fraught admission of the perversion of his sex instinct and of the impulses which led him to satisfy his sexual passions by abnormal means. It is only rarely that the medico-legal expert can obtain the intimate journals of such individuals, their correspondence or other interesting documents, as we see from the classic treatises of Casper and of Tardieu.

But these diaries and autobiographies are stamped to the utmost with the fault common to all productions of this sort, that is the desire to arouse sympathy and set off in relief only their good sides. In this way the description becomes exaggerated, unfaithful, and profoundly misleading.

The clinician, on the contrary, does not have prisoners to examine. The patient comes to him spontaneously to get his advice, he expects assistance from the doctor, and confides his trouble to him down to the slightest details. There is no room in such a case for premeditated deceit or conscious lying. That is why the clinician is in a position to distinguish the initial symptoms of an anomaly or disease, to follow its development, and observe its progress over a period of years. He thus obtains a comprehensive, coherent view of the disorder.

Two categories of medical specialists are most frequently consulted by the patients we are here concerned with, namely the neuropathologists and those who treat genital affections. The persons who have recourse to the first are principally those in whom there exist well defined symptoms accompanied by perversion of the sexual instinct. The disorder of the procreative activity is here merely an accessory in the series of graver phenomena which overwhelm the patient. Specialists in mental diseases have, in addition, facilities in their asylums for observing the terminal forms of those affections which manifest themselves at the start in perversion of the procreative power, and end up in absolute madness.

Specialists in diseases of the genital organs are consulted by persons who notice even slight signs of some organic anomaly, of an arrested development, or premonitory indications of an incipient disease in which diminution of sexual potency is the most outstanding symptom, or finally, when syphilitic infection makes inevitable the avowal of some perversion of the genital instinct.

Among those consulting him, the specialist finds the young man who, arrived at the age of virility, realizes that he is absolutely impotent with women, and confusedly perceives in himself certain abnormal sexual leanings; the old man whose sexual activity has long since disappeared, but who all of a sudden experiences a new drive of the senses, an exaggerated lust, and morbid stimulation of desire; the husband who adores his wife and periodically yields to the invincible sexual urge, but who feels himself carried away into performing the conjugal act in a totally unaccustomed, repugnant manner; the voluptuary who has become aware of a decline in his sexual potency, and who does not know whether to think it a quantitative or qualitative change in the function.

Such are the persons who seek first aid and advice from the specialist in diseases of the reproductive organs. It is to him, too, that the habitual pederast comes and makes his voluntary confession when he has through misfortune suffered syphilitic contamination. To him comes the young boy lately seduced, who finds himself prey to some disorder of the anus or rectum. The confession of their failing is generally a source of great moral mortification to these patients. They often make it in writing, surrounding themselves with precautions to insure the mystery and secret, and a frank confession can be obtained only if the physician takes an unreproving attitude and declares himself ready to lend his support.

I may also call attention to the fact that nearly all pederasts, whatever class they belong to, are more or less known to one another, at least in large cities, and that they generally seek the advice of the same doctor. Because of this the doctor's task in eliciting sincere, frank admissions on the subject of genital anomalies is considerably facilitated. In the course of my twenty-five years of medical practice I have had particularly to deal with the various phases of diseases affecting the genital organs. As I have made all my observations carefully, I have been able to get together a vast collection of facts bearing upon morbid manifestations of the reproductive sense.

The confirmed criminal and the real lunatic are two extremes between which we find a multitude of sick men whose condition is not recognized, and of vicious subjects burdened with some abnormal functioning of the reproductive power. It is the latter of these two groups which will furnish the most abundant material for the studies which are to follow.

My observations have been made not upon prisoners at the bar, not from the records of insane asylums, but upon persons constituting part of society at large, persons sound of mind and in full possession of their legal rights. I believe that these observations may bring forth new conceptions directed toward sharp differentiation between vice and disease, between congenital taint and moral defection.

It was my intention to treat the subject so as to render it intelligible not only to the physician, but also to the man of law. Therefore its exposition has come to considerable length, in view of the digressions necessary to ensure maximum understanding. I am convinced that it is only by a scrupulous investigation of what we call offenses against public morality, and by methodic exposition of the facts, as compared with ordinary legal practice, that we may enable jurists fully informed on the present knowledge regarding morbid manifestations of the sexual instinct to arrive at just conclusions.

CHAPTER ONE

The Various Types of Pederasts

THE sexual instinct manifests itself in the human being prior to fully developed maturity, and in the healthy
individual is translated into a feeling of attraction toward persons of the opposite sex. This attraction is
soon transformed into conscious desire to accomplish
the sexual act, and if the desire keeps on growing, it
may attain the state of an uninterrupted sexual need.

Among anomalies of the reproductive functions, perversion of the sexual instinct is most distinctly evinced
by morbid inclination toward persons of the same sex.
In men, who are almost the exclusive subject of this
study, this form of sexual perversion is designated by
the general name of "pederasty".[1] We shall see later
that bestiality and sodomy are merely varieties of the
above-mentioned abnormal sexual impulse.

---

1. From two Greek words παιδὸς ἐραστής, that is to say *pueri
   amator*, better known by the Romans under the name of
   "Greek love".

9

Relations of Pederasty to Other Perversions

Manifestations of pederasty constitute the most definite and best studied group of sexual aberrations, for it is they that most often give rise to judicial inquests. That is why the most considerable portion of this work is devoted to pederasty taken in the broadest sense of the word. There is, however, no need for this study to be concerned solely with the vice in question, without at the same time considering its relations to other forms of sexual perversion. We shall therefore examine the latter as well, in so far as that is useful for the clarification of the subject.

Since pederasty develops under the influence of widely diversified causes, we must divide it, like all other aberrations of the genital sense, into several groups and species quite different from one another. This division must be made according to the clinical and etiological points of view.

Morbid manifestations of sexual activity are first of all divided into two large groups, according to whether they develop in subjects predisposed from birth to these aberrations and to nervous disorders of any sort, or on the contrary, whether they appear in individuals relatively sound, without hereditary taint. In the *first group,* disorder of reproductive functions must be attributed to psychopathic or neuropathic temperament, whereas in the *second group* we have to do with individuals who from birth onward have always been in possession of a well-constituted normal nervous system.

The symptoms which arise from an hereditary infirmity are likewise revealed in various forms. In some cases they show themselves with the first awakening of the reproductive instinct, and their evolution remains impervious to the influence of education or example, reaching its maximum intensity at the time of sexual maturity and virility, and persisting throughout life with alternate periods of diminution and increase.

These aberrations are of constant, invariable nature, and are just as peculiar to the individual organism as other innate personal peculiarities of character, sentiments, or morals. It is these disorders constituting the first kind of hereditary infirmity which we shall assemble under the name of *innate perversion of the sexual instinct,* and in this group we shall include *innate pederasty.*

To the second division of the same group belong those alterations of reproductive activity which are from time to time manifested, *nolens volens,* in the form of morbid attacks. These attacks are separated by intervals during which the sexual functions are performed in normal fashion. The general name of *periodic perversion of the sexual instinct,* and the particular denomination of *periodic pederasty,* appear to me most fitting to designate these morbid disorders. They agree perfectly with what we call *periodic psychoses,* more pronounced manifestations of psychic degeneration, revealed by occasional seizures of mental derangement, although between attacks there exist long intervals during which the mental faculties give proof of relatively normal activity.

In a third division of sexual disorders, I put the disturbances seen in the morbid phenomena well-known under the general name of epilepsy. Among the mental disturbances which spring up in the course of this disease, there may become manifest a sort of psychic epilepsy expressed in pederasty.

I regard as paroxystic phenomena, analogous to hysteria and mania, the morbid manifestations of the sexual instinct observed in satyriasis and erotomania. The description of the latter concludes the group of perturbations based upon hereditary taint.

The second group comprises all aberrations of sexual activity which may be the result of education or example, or which are born spontaneously from some personal impulse, whether it be the expression of vicious inclination or voluntary depravity. In our opinion, the terms *acquired perversion of the sexual functions,* and *acquired pederasty,* best answer the category of facts included in this group. Various subdivisions in this group correspond to such disturbances of the sexual functions as reveal disease in process of development, affecting either the nervous centres or the whole organism, disease which seizes upon subjects whose brain has from childhood on always been soundly constituted. We must also include the sexual perversions characteristic of senile decrepitude, *senile pederasty,* and the sexual aberrations observed in the initial stage of paralytic idiocy, *paralytic pederasty.*

Every man who studies nature knows that a division into groups based upon a particular symptom is purely conventional and artificial, serves but to facilitate research, and does not rest upon a fixed, impregnable organic foundation. So it is with the classification I propose. It must undergo modification from contact with living reality. The different forms and types gradually merge, become mutually involved, take on new shades of color and appearance, in accordance with the complexity of forms of sexual aberrations, forms which we are going to describe in distinct groups.

Lastly, I have striven to determine the conceptions that may serve to establish a differential diagnosis for the various groups and classes of sexual aberrations. We shall begin by describing the forms most frequently encountered.

CHAPTER TWO

Voluptuous Strangeness of Pederasty

JUST as children may be born with anomalies of the extremities, trunk, head or other members, so there may be revealed a congenital tendency towards perverted modes of expressing the sexual instinct. Though an individual be afflicted with a physical deformity, the rest of the organism, aside from the particular anomaly, may be more or less normally developed. Similarly, a person who bears some moral malformation may have a more or less normal psychic constitution, if we except the particular perversion which concerns us. Irregular or defective development of the nervous centres may show a special character, limiting the functional disturbance to a particular field, that of sexual activity, for example. But the defective development of certain nervous centres is not without influence upon that of others. It is generally possible to recognize in a malformation (despite the more or

15

less regular constitution of the parts of the body which are not directly affected) a series of slight deviations and irregularities, perhaps not apparent upon superficial examination, but nevertheless disclosed by attentive study. Likewise, where there exists a limited congenital disorder of the nervous centres, the result is a certain influence upon the whole nervous system, betrayed by irregularities which are difficult to perceive. Therefore to obtain a general view of the anomaly in question, together with all related irregularities, it is necesary to follow its general development from the very earliest manifestations.

The child born with a congenital sexual perversion grows up and develops in a manner which appears absolutely regular. Only the sexual instinct awakens in an abnormally precocious way, and when the period of sexual maturity approaches, a whole series of manifestations make their entry on the scene. The first of these symptoms is an expression of shame, not before young girls or women, but in the presence of adult men. For example, the young boy experiences more shame in undressing before a strange man than before a woman.

On the other hand, he prefers the company and caresses of men to those of women. He feels a great attachment to a man, follows him everywhere unceasingly, obeys him without a murmur, is captivated by his charm, in short is in love with the man, be he good, generous, clever or merely vigorously muscled, whereas women leave him completely indifferent. Finally he reaches puberty; at night he often has violent erections with emission of sperm. The pollutions are accompanied by dreams, at first vague and easily forgotten, but each time they become more and more distinct, more sharply outlined, astonishing the young man by their strange character. It is not feminine caresses or encounters with women that make up the subject of his dreams, but pressings of the hand and kisses exchanged with grown men, well-built and handsome. In the dream, the final erection followed by ejaculation is provoked not by a woman's form in seductive attitudes and movements, but by the embraces, caresses and kisses of men.

Not only does the representation of the feminine form give rise to no sexual excitation, but moreover it paralyzes every voluptuous feeling that may happen to be present. In men normally constituted the intensity of sexual erethism rapidly abates at sight of other adult men. In the congenital pederast, on the contrary, this excitation suddenly dies away in the presence of women. The sight of a naked woman leaves him unmoved, while that of a naked man awakens in him sensations of desire.

Books and talks with his comrades have made him understand that something extraordinary, something abnormal is taking place within him. But the strangeness presented by this internal phenomenon, the difficulty of defining it, and his constantly growing timidity in

the company of men, cause the young man to dissimulate his misfortune. Sometimes, urged on by companions of his own age, he ventures to share the bed of a
young girl, and attempts to perform the virile act, but
each time his efforts fail, and it is not rare for them
to be followed by a fit of hysteria.

Just as a man normally constituted and developed
from the sexual point of view is unable, whatever efforts he makes, to feel licentious desire for another
man, so it is perfectly impossible for the congenital
pederast to accomplish coitus with a woman. These
futile efforts serve still more to discourage the young
man, and finally inspire in him a disgust for women.
Then he seeks out the company of men, courts them,
becomes enamored of them, and at the same time seeks
to satisfy himself by onanism. In consequence of the
congenital morbid erethism, the lascivious sensations
quickly reach their maximum intensity, and often mere
physical contact with the beloved person will suffice
to provoke seminal emission.

Love in these subjects is extraordinarily violent, pathologically passionate, absorbing all moral and emotional faculties. In the beginning it is purely platonic;
the sexual sense, with its fleshly urge, finds satisfaction only later in mutual masturbation, or in onanism
provoked by the thought of the adored person. Finally, when the latter consents to it, or to satisfy the desire
in another fashion, they practice sodomy, in which case

the morbidly disposed subject always fills the role of passive pederast.

Concurrently with the exaggeration of sexual perversion we have just described, there appear other peculiarities bearing witness to the disorder of the organism. The young man shows a propensity for giving himself a feminine air, he likes to don women's attire, to curl his hair, to go about with his throat exposed and waist drawn in, to perfume himself, to apply powder and rouge, to paint his eyebrows, etc. Thus is produced a type of man with feminine allurements, who disgusts individuals of his own sex, whom women look upon with contempt, and who is at once recognized by his appearance.

Generally they are of medium size or slight in build, have broad hips, narrow shoulders, affect women's walk with a particular swaying gait. Their curly hair scented, dressed in eccentric fashion, with bracelets on the wrists, they seek by every means—laughter, words, gestures — to attract the attention of men to themselves. The unhappy wretch, especially if his intellect is relatively underdeveloped, fails to realize that the more he strives to imitate women, the more repugnant he becomes to normal men. Fanciful to the point of hysteria, envious, cowardly, mediocre, vindictive, hateful, he unites in himself all of women's faults, and possesses none of those traits which arouse love for the male character. They are equally despicable to men and to women. Many of these sick persons voluntarily recognize their abnormal state, which they endeavor to explain by saying, "I have a woman's soul in a man's body", in the words of K. H. Ulrichs.[1] The latter produced a whole series of treatises, which despite their interest as the detailed confessions of a psychopath, are none the less confused and dragged out like most works of this sort.

It often happens that these sufferers are quite overcome by the discovery of their infirmity and their inability to combat it. A letter kindly communicated to us by Professor J. Mierzejewsky is of the highest interest in this connection. This is its purport: " .... To speak frankly, even here at a distance, I am exposed to temptations against which I am defenceless, and I really do not know what the meaning is. Is it disease, the power of youthful impressions, or lack of will, that I have been vainly fighting for more than four years? Or else, is it an unhappy nature, a fatal destiny, an instinct which death alone may cure? That is why at times I dream of a quick poison which would not make me suffer, because in reality my own judgment is opposed to this instinct .... "

Some months before his marriage with a charming young girl, one of my patients wrote me the following: "I am a slave to a fatal passion, I cannot give up my vice, and I am incapable of loving Miss X ... although

---

1. Numa Numantius (pseudonym of the celebrated Karl Ulrichs): *Anthropologische Studien über die mannmännliche Geschlechtsliebe*; Leipzig, 1869.

I feel that it is with her alone that I could be happy. In her absence, I am in love with her mind, her spirit, her very face, but when I see her, I feel that I am in no condition to become her husband . . . That would be the greatest of misfortunes. Until now I have never been able to have intercourse with a woman; it would be the same with her . . . All that remains for me is to die, if your assistance proves ineffective . . . . "

Sometimes the sick man, tortured with the jealousy inspired by women's successes with men, falls into despair over his almost always unhappy loves. Often repulsed with scorn, he may kill himself in a fit of melancholy, or sinking lower and lower, may confine himself to the narrow circle of a few companions in misery, ending his days in a state of semi-senselessness. Or else he becomes the victim of one form or other of acute madness, unless his miserable life is previously terminated by some inter-current malady. The type described here combines in itself the principal characteristics of the congenital pederast, such as we most frequently encounter.

There are others, however, who in their efforts to imitate the fair sex, adopt queerer forms. Thus, for example, Taylor[1] has written a most important observation where he describes the celebrated English actress and adventuress, Elisa Edwards, who after her death was recognized to have been a man in disguise. From

---

1. *Medical Jurisprudence*, 1873. Vol. II, pp. 286 and 473.

his earliest youth he felt a leaning towards men. After the age of fourteen, he wore women's clothes, entered the theatre, had numerous lovers and amorous adventures. He was in the habit of keeping his quite normally developed genitals pressed close against the body by means of a special bandage, so as not to be recognized.

Despite the very clearly expressed inclination to copy the female sex in the above case, the sexual perversion indicated does not really differ from that revealed in the previously described type of the passive congenital pederast, called "*cinaedus*" (catamite).

But aside from cases like this there exist other intermediate forms presented under conditions which we must now define; morbid aberrations, more or less strongly marked, which constitute a gradual transition towards evident types of hereditary mental derangement. In the less accentuated manifestations, the little boy or young man only reveals his predisposition by devoting himself to women's occupations. He is fond of knitting, sewing, making doll's clothes; or again, he distinguishes himself by his predilection for feminine manners, striving to be graceful and coquettish in his demeanor, imitating the tone and voice of a woman, etc. When he talks with men he blushes, feels awkward, out-of-place. In the company of young girls, however, he is quite free from embarrassment, is happy to play the woman's part when dancing, always chooses a vigorous, solid-bodied male-dancer as partner, becomes quite animated and joyous when he has found a man of his taste, or else may even be confused and troubled at his sight, running away like a timid young girl.

Another spends all his leisure time in front of a mirror combing his hair, applying curl-papers, rouging his face, adorning his person, seriously studying what becomes him, and what is unbecoming to him. He possesses an amazing memory for the most complicated women's apparel and can describe them in all their details. He gives proof of exceptionally delicate taste in this field, but when he adopts men's clothes, he reveals himself as quite devoid of taste. For example, he displays a tie of too violent color, or allows his throat to be seen so far down that even in a woman it would seem exaggerated, or else he wears his hair in long, curly locks, covers his fingers with rings and puts bracelets on his wrists.

In other less pronounced forms, the sexual instinct is often determined by the influence of surrounding conditions. When the teachers or parents of such morbid individuals fail to understand the significance of the manifestations described above, accord them slight attention, or even, for fun, encourage these feminine traits, the inevitable result is that the morbidly predisposed young man becomes an onanist. He does not feel attracted towards women, draws further and further away from them, and finally, when a favorable occasion arises, becomes a pederast, although at the start he still retained the power to have sexual relations with women. The more intense these morbid manifestations are, the longer the subject gives himself up to masturbation, the sooner he becomes a pederast, the sooner he loses the aptitude for normal coition.

More fatal still in its effects upon predisposed beings is life in common with comrades bearing a similar taint, more advanced pathologically, as often occurs in schools. Through the example of older comrades, the young boy early becomes a pederast, and because of this, when puberty arrives, the morbid diminution in his desire for women is still more accentuated.

Under more favorable conditions the case presents a better conclusion. When the young boy has been curbed in time, when his first feminine imitations have been derided, he himself begins involuntarily to turn away from them. If, subsequently, he is kept carefully removed from the company of women, occupied as much as possible with athletic exercises, always severely reprimanded and punished for the slightest indication of coquettry, exaggerated delicacy, or other outward sign of effeminacy, this strictly guided education will lead to normal puberty. The congenitally morbid diminution in the sexual appetite for women, together with the weakening and perversion of the reproductive instinct—consequences of bad environment and defective education—cause the young man in this initial stage of his life to be more indifferent to sexual pleasure than comrades of the same age. It often happens that when he has attained the age of virility, his first relations with women fail, or else despite their consummation, he does not meet with the same enjoyment in them as would a normally constituted being. However, if he perseveres in having regular contacts, especially with the same person, the young man inherently predisposed to perversion becomes a man endowed with normal genital functions, fit to fulfill his duties as head of a family.

Another variety of these morbid manifestations is that of the cases where touching of the posterior brings about sexual erethism, whose satisfaction is not perverted and may be met with in the normal state. Sometimes the young boy has noticed in his early childhood that light taps on his uncovered bottom cause him an agreeable sensation.[1] After that, while playing, amusing himself, or even as punishment, he voluntarily seeks to have a few slaps administered. When this particular predisposition is not recognized, blows especially provoke an erotic excitation in the child. Later on, he flogs himself when alone, and the excitation concludes in onanism. When the period of virility arrives, if the vicious habit of seeking excitement through flagellation (that is blows with rods on the posterior region) has become deeply rooted, the patient can only have intercourse with women after having been previously flagellated, which deprives him

---

1. J. J. Rousseau: Confessions, part I, book I.

forever of family life, and necessarily reduces him to
having recourse to masturbation or the exclusive fre-
quenting of prostitutes. Under these conditions the vicious propensity is pushed still further. Blows alone,
even carried to the point of bloodshed, do not suffice
the sufferer; he demands that violence be used upon
him. He must be brutally undressed, they must tie his
wrists together, fasten him to a bench, etc., during
which he offers feigned resistance, cries out and curses.
It is only by such means, in addition to flagellation,
that he succeeds in attaining the degree of venereal
excitation which terminates in the seminal emission.
At this period of morbidity, he rarely arrives at real
coition; more frequently the semen is spilt without
even an erection. Finally the patient loses completely
the faculty for normal performance of the sexual
function, and shows gradual development of predisposition to graver forms of nervous and mental disease.

It goes without saying that when the morbid propensity is discovered early, and when abnormal excitation
from touching of the posterior is carefully avoided,
the period of puberty is much retarded, and efforts to
overcome the congenital infirmity become easier and
more fruitful.

CHAPTER THREE

Curiosities of Pederastic Desire

BESIDES the attenuated congenital forms which indicate a more or less mild disposition to pederasty, there are others more violent, fortunately less common, which show a gradual transition to complete madness. Several of these subjects find their first lustful sensations excited by the sight of a nude man, particularly of his posterior, or of the anal orifice. Doctor Albert,[1] in confirmation of cases where schoolmasters have without reason flogged their pupils, cites the view of the bare bottoms of the children as producing in these teachers a state of sensual excitement which they later satisfy by masturbation. When such subjects become early addicts to masturbation, they seek to excite themselves by touching the posteriors of men, or by rubbing up against them, and in these circumstances there is often a spermatic emission. They also have nocturnal

---

1. Albert: *Friedreich's Blätter*, 1859, III, p. 77.

pollutions accompanied by dreams, in which naked men with strongly developed buttocks play the principal role. Such individuals are born active pederasts. They are always indifferent to women, have no feminine proclivities, but usually, aside from their sexual perversion, reveal other equally morbid symptoms, bearing witness to degeneration in more or less degree. Some, from childhood on, display a tendency to thieving, which cannot be explained by neediness. Others are subject to epileptic seizures with momentary loss of consciousness. Still others are afflicted with intellectual laziness, any mental effort quickly fatigues them, their understanding is slow, their memory poor, and so on.

One step further in psychic degeneration and we reach those subjects who have a taste exclusively for old men. Many born pederasts feel attracted only toward men with grey beards. For them, neither youth, nor elegance of form, nor beauty, whether masculine or feminine, possesses any importance whatever. Their sexual instinct can be excited only before a greybeard, at times even with the ugliest face, rendered repulsive by deformity.

Another phase of this congenital perversion is manifested in those individuals in whom sexual excitation is provoked by the sight of inanimate objects having no relation whatever to the sex act. There are cases known where the sight of a night-cap on the head of a man or woman has provoked an erethism with emission of sperm. The sight of the naked body of a woman or of a man left the subject unmoved, but the memory of a night-cap, particularly on the head of an old woman, all wrinkled, or contact with a night-cap, immediately brought on erection and even ejaculation.

One unfortunate patient was accustomed at an early age to direct his attention to the nails in women's boots. The contemplation of boots so supplied with nails procured him a very special pleasure. He would get up at night, secretly hunt up shoes of this kind, then stretching out on his bed, would abandon himself to all sorts of fantastic imaginings in which the nailed boots would cause erection. In this way he fell into precocious onanism. Later on, the mere sight of a shoemaker driving nails into the soles of the patient's own boots would suffice to make him ejaculate without erection.

In a third case, the initial genital erethism was caused by the view of a white apron hung out in the sunlight to dry. The patient detached the apron, held it in front of himself and began to masturbate. From that time on the sight of a white apron always provoked an erethism in him. It was indifferent to him whether the apron was worn by a man or by a woman, or merely hanging on a line for drying clothes; the sight of the apron invariably awakened in him the irresistible desire to take possession of it and masturbate with it. Punished several times for stealing aprons, he entered a monastery where of his own initiative he sought to conquer the flesh by fasting and prayer, but he was unable to conquer his passion, and the recollection of white aprons was enough to make him fall back again into his vice.

Another subject experienced violent desire, terminated by spasmodic erection, when his genital organs came into contact with fur. That was produced once by chance, on a night when he had to cover himself with a fur blanket. From that time on—he was then twelve years old—he gave himself up to masturbation. The sight of the body of a man or woman, even during copulation, did not in the least excite him, but contact with the hair of a small dog which he sometimes took to bed, always brought about an erection terminating in seminal emission, the latter being at times followed by an attack of hysteria accompanied with convulsions, sobbing, etc. The nocturnal pollutions were concomitant with dreams in which neither men nor women took part. Generally he dreamt that he was stretched out stark naked on a soft fur-piece which at every point pressed amorously against his body, and this sensation led to the erection and pollution. Having grown older and persuaded of his morbid state, he was really desperate at times, and was often on the verge of resorting to suicide. He was very quickly fatigued by mental work and failed in his university examinations. His memory grew much feebler. It seemed to him that

---

1.　Charcot and Magnan. Inversion du sens génital. *Arch. de Neurologie*, 1882.

his comrades looked at him in a peculiar way and had contempt for him. It was this last point that troubled him most of all. He was in the habit of asking himself whether they were able to diagnose his condition by the expression of his eyes, whether there was not some means, by taking remedies, of hiding his situation from them. He cried out, wept, suffered terribly, begged to be saved from himself. "If I should find out that they guess what is taking place within me, I would most certainly kill myself!" These were the words he addressed to me on leaving, at the time of our last interview. Evidently the persecution mania was already developing in him. I have since learned that some months later he had been placed in an insane asylum.

This patient showed degeneration in advanced degree. His genital organs were irregularly developed, and his bony structure presented evident malformations. Just the same way, in all the previously cited cases, aside from a high degree of perversion of the sex instinct, we have observed other manifestations pointing to abnormal development of the nervous system due to degeneration. The night-cap patient had hallucinations at times; he was prone to melancholy and had frequently evinced the intention of poisoning himself. The patient in whom erethism was provoked by the sight of boot-nails also had fits of hysteria or hypochondriasis, was subject to hallucinations, and so on. The lover of the white aprons had from childhood on been inclined to thieving, and had only superficial understanding of things. Later on he was prey to melancholic seizures with ideas of suicide. At the same time he showed somatic stigmata of degeneration: the skull was irregularly constituted and presented characteristic deformation.

Dr. Krauss[1] reports a similar case in which stealing did not have a criminal aim, but simply served to satisfy a perverted sexual instinct. This observation .is borrowed from Eulenberg[2] and concerns a subject aged 45, of fiery malicious nature. "Often there were produced in him phenomena which he did not understand; his head would become heavy, hot as if ready to burn up. He was unable to think or work, and experienced a need for running about like a dog. At these moments he submitted to an irresistible urge to steal women's lingerie wherever he might find it. He was never troubled by fear of being caught. Moreover, he never stole any other objects, nor money. He was in the habit of putting on these linens, sometimes during the day, but more often he would go to bed at night after having slipped them on. To put them on and wear them produced voluptuous sensations in him, and his semen would be involuntarily spilt.... He neither sold nor gave away a single one of the articles stolen, but put them all aside in cupboards, trunks, even in his mattresses, and other hiding places. When he was arrest-

1. A. Krauss: *Die Psychologie des Verbrechens*. Tübingen, 1884, p. 190.
2. Eulenberg: *Vierteljahresschr. f. Gerichtl. Medizin*. 1878, Bd. 28.

ed, he was wearing several articles of women's apparel, and next his body he wore a woman's chemise. At his home they found principally women's step-ins and chemises, corsets, brassieres, stockings, handkerchiefs, a total of three hundred articles." In no case did he steal linens from young women and girls of his acquaintance. He never knew the persons to whom these stolen linens belonged. His sexual instinct was directed toward the female elements within himself. All other sexual aberrations seem to have been absent. There was neither onanism, nor pederasty, nor lascivious amusements in the company of young boys. But the desire for women, in the way of normal sexual satisfaction, did not exist either. He admits furthermore that for a long time he had had no relations with women, but asserts that formerly he was capable of accomplishing coitus. Some years ago he had been engaged, but the marriage had been broken off by the parents of his intended wife. This had deeply grieved him.

Opposite this observation we may add another by Diez[1] relative to a young boy who experienced an unconquerable urge to tear women's garments, an act always followed by spermatic emission.

An example very well studied from the point of view of the etiology of congenital sexual perversion has recently been reported by Professor Lombroso. He sets forth the case of a young man of twenty who inherited

---

1. E. A. Diez: *Der Selbstmord*, 1838, p. 24.

a psychopathic tendency from his immediate ancestors, his grandfather died insane, his mother suffered from migraine, his sister was hysterical, one of his brothers is a stammerer, and a cousin is half idiotic. Already having such predispositions, the patient furthermore injured his head in infancy, and for a long time thereafter suffered as a result of it. Since childhood he had likewise been subject to intercostal pains and pains in the hip region. From his third or fourth year he had had erections and violent excitations at sight of white objects, even white walls, but principally at sight of linen hanging out to dry. Touching linens or hearing their rustling aroused erotic sensations. From his ninth or tenth year on he had always masturbated upon seeing starched white linen. Although he possessed well-developed faculties and a desire to learn he left school at the age of nine, stole money from his parents, several times set fire to their house, was frequently arrested for street-brawls and carrying prohibited weapons, and was finally sentenced to death for murder.[1]

---

1. Lombroso: Amori anomali e precoci nei pazzie. *Arch. di psich. sc. pen.*, 1883, IV, p.17.

CHAPTER FOUR

Sexual Crimes of European Perverts

It is easy to understand how, aside from well-determined psychic and physical anomalies, successive degrees of degeneration may also present still more debased forms of sexual perversion, such as the impulse to torture victims, to wound them, to see their blood flow, or even the desire to violate little children. Elsewhere, the lewd desire finds complete satisfaction only in the disfiguring or killing of the victim, in swallowing portions of the flesh, or performing the sex act upon the dead body. In this connection there are two observations by Demme[1] which are of the highest interest, because they present two different degrees of the same sexual perversion.

The first observation is as follows: Carl Battle, a wine-merchant in Augsburg, 37 years of age, had never in his life had intercourse with women. He had, on the

---

1. See Krauss, p. 183.

contrary, always felt repulsion for them. And yet the sex instinct was very powerful in him. At the age of nineteen he was for the first time assailed by the invincible need to inflict slight wounds upon young girls, an act which seemed to procure him a sort of sexual pleasure. Therefore he slightly injured several girls and each time had a seminal emission. But after such an act, he would always reproach himself, would feel a kind of remorse and would make a resolution to master his impulse. At first he confined himself to making little cuts, taking care not to wound the little girls seriously. Later on he was led to clutch the arms or throat of young girls whom he encountered. But that did not suffice to satisfy the sexual urge; it brought about erection, it is true, but not ejaculation. More serious injuries became necessary. He began to prick his victims with a stiletto. Curiously enough, if the girl's clothes had saved her from injury, he always found that his attempt had remained fruitless, for he then had no emission of sperm.

Besides, the wound must not be dangerous; he was too religious for that. He chose his victims among pretty girls only, completely sparing older women. He never went in for onanism, although his nocturnal dreams, filled with young wounded girls, led to ejaculation.

In his dwelling-place they found a collection of finely-wrought stilettos, sword-canes, poniards, hunting-knives, etc. He stated with respect to them that for a long time he had felt a desire to possess such arms.

Pleasure from Genital Knife Wounds

The mere sight of them, and better still, the contact of
their naked gleaming blades, produced in him voluptuous sensations accompanied by violent erections. According to information given by those who knew him,
he was a man of very peaceful character, loving sol-
itude and always having an aversion for the company
of women. His appearance was pleasing, and he enjoyed honest affluence. It was discovered that before
his arrest he had perpetrated fifty attacks upon young
girls. Besides the stiletto, he used lancets and embroid-
ery-needles as weapons.

Demme's[1] second observation has to do with a soldier
named Xaver, of Botzen (Tyrol). This patient found
special delight in inflicting knife-wounds upon the hid-
den parts of young girls whom he might meet in the
streets, then in watching the blood drip from the knife
blade. According to the statements he made in court,
this procured him the same pleasure as he might have
had in performing the sex act with his victim.

Xaver was from childhood on addicted to masturbation. He regularly frequented prostitutes and besides,
had often practised sodomy with little girls. Later, he
experienced particular pleasure when masturbating in
sight of little girls who "watched him with quite inno-
cent curiosity." In such cases he was dominated by the
idea: "How delicious it would be to cut the intimate
parts of little girls with a knife, and watch the blood

---

1.   Krauss, p.181.

trickling drop by drop from the blade!" According to him, this wanton impulse, "inspired by the devil", was unconquerable, and after each attempt it became more furious, and more impossible to restrain. In this way he had wounded seven young girls, and was not more than thirty years old when arrested.

According to the depositions of his comrades and superiors, Xaver was of an ardent temperament, but in no way a bad man. He presented remarkable singularities, was always extremely reserved, and would often remain for hours in contemplation of paintings of religious character.

The following case is an instance of more pronounced sexual perversion in the same direction: A young man of 24 entices a little girl of 12 into a wood, begins by violating her, then kills her. He drinks her blood, cuts up her sexual parts as well as her heart, and concludes by devouring them. His crime having been proven, he acknowledged his guilt and was executed.[1]

A similar case, in which a man suffering a cerebral affection was deliberately condemned to death, has been recently met with in France. In 1880 a young man of 19 named Menesclou was executed in Paris. He enticed a little girl of 4 to his room, had raped her, strangled her, then cut her body into pieces. To the misfortune and shame of science, the experts in psychopathology who were in charge, Lasègue, Brouardel

---

1. See Krafft-Ebing: *Arch. f. Psych.*, 1877, p.296.

and Motet, despite the grave and evident psychic degeneration displayed by the accused, gave out an unfavorable verdict. They declared him responsible for his acts, and the sick man was guillotined. The examination of Menesclou's brain in an anthropological laboratory demonstrated that the two frontal lobes, the first and second temporal circumvolutions, and the occipital circumvolution were in a state of softening.[1]

Blumröder[2] and Lombroso[3] have noted several anthropological cases where, according to the patients' statements, coition was far from satisfying them. Their lust was completely sated only when they had assassinated their victims, torn them to pieces, probed their entrails, and even eaten portions of them.

---

1. See the Affaire Menesclou in the *Annales d'Hygiène Publique*, 1880, p.439.
2. Blumröder: Ueber Lust und Schmerz. *Friedreich's Magas. f. Seelen.*, 1830, II, 2.
3. Lombroso: Monograph on "Verzeni e Agnolette". Rome, 1874.

CHAPTER FIVE

Staggering Lust Crimes of French

Sergeant Bertrand: Detailed Confessions

ONE remarkable example of necrophily is the well-known case of Sergeant Bertrand, a handsome young man of 25, of sympathetic appearance, who was in the habit of exhuming female corpses in cemeteries, and violating them.[1] In his confession written in prison before his execution, Bertrand says among other things[2]: "From my earliest childhood, I masturbated without knowing what I was doing. I did it openly, without hiding myself. Towards the age of 8 to 10, I began to think of women. The desire for them developed in me only towards my thirteenth or fourteenth year. Then I knew no more restraint and masturbated seven or eight times a day. The mere sight of an article of feminine attire was enough to cause an erection. During the act of masturbation my imagination transported me to a

---

1. S. Michea: *Union médicale*, 1849.
2. Tardieu: *Attentats aux moeurs*, Paris, 1875, p.114.

room full of women, all at my disposal. I would in my mind torture them in every possible way, according to my desire. I would imagine them as dead before me, and would defile their corpses. Sometimes the idea would come to me to dismember the body of a man, but that was rare, and it disgusted me.

"....Not having the means for procuring human corpses, I sought the dead bodies of animals, upon which I perpetrated atrocities like those I later committed upon corpses of men and women. I would open the belly, tear out the entrails, and while gazing on them, I would masturbate. Then I would retire, filled with shame at my conduct, promising myself never to begin again, but my passion was stronger than my will. By behaving this way I enjoyed an indescribable voluptuousness.

"....In 1846, I was no longer able to satisfy myself with the dead bodies of animals. I needed living subjects. Around the Villette encampment, and many other camps, there were numerous stray dogs who followed the soldiers. I decided to attract a few outside the town-walls and kill them there. I succeeded two or three times, dismembered them as I had previously done with animal corpses, and obtained the same enjoyment.

"It was towards the end of 1846 that the idea first came to me to disinter human corpses. What made me think of it was the ease with which one could snatch a dead body from the common pit in cemeteries. But I did not do it then; fear held me back. At the beginning of 1847 the regiment was ordered to move on to Tours, and my detachment remained in the little town of Béré. It is there that I achieved my first profanation of a corpse under the following circumstances. It was about noon. I was walking with a comrade just outside the town and out of curiosity we entered the cemetery that lay in our path. It was nearly the end of February. The night before, someone had been buried, and rain having fallen, the grave had not been disturbed, the pick and spade had been left behind. This sight awakened the most sacrilegious thoughts in me. I had a violent headache, my heart began to palpitate, I could no longer contain myself. By pretext I sought to return immediately to town. No sooner had I left my comrade than I came back to the cemetery, and without being uneasy because of some husbandmen busy in a neighboring vineyard, I seized the spade and with truly extraordinary strength began to dig up the grave. As soon as I encountered the body, having no sharp-edged instrument at hand for cutting it up, I set about striking it with the spade, using all my might, and with a rage that I cannot even explain.

" . . . . Arriving in Douai some time after this incident, I again enjoyed the pleasure of dismembering a corpse. The night of March 10th, I came to the cemetery. It was nine o'clock. After the eight o'clock tattoo no soldier had the right to go beyond the town limits. Therefore I had to scale a high wall and cross a ditch by swimming. The cold was intense and pieces of ice floated on the water. But these obstacles did not stop me. When I arrived at the cemetery, I dug up the corpse of a girl from 15 to 17 years of age. There, for the first time, I gave myself up to the mad embrace of a dead body. I cannot describe my sensations, but all the joy procured by possession of a living woman was as nothing in comparison with the pleasure I felt. I showered kisses upon all parts of her body, pressed her to my heart with a madman's frenzy. I overwhelmed her with the most passionate caresses. After having regaled myself with this pleasure for a quarter of an hour I started to cut the body open and pull out the entrails, as I had done with all the other victims of my madness. Then I replaced the body in the grave, covered it lightly with earth, and returned to the barracks by the same road I had come.

" .... I have always liked to destroy things. During my childhood my parents refrained from buying me anything at all, for I was sure to break it to pieces. Having grown up, I could never preserve an object, a knife for example, for more than two weeks without breaking it, and even now I experience the same urge to destroy. If I buy a pipe, it is broken the same evening or next morning, at the latest. While still with the regiment, it has often happened that returning somewhat drunk, I have broken everything that fell into my hands."

In a letter written subsequently by Bertrand to Marchal de Calvis we read: "Concerning the erotic monomania, I maintain that it was not preceded by the destructive impulse. It was only in the month of May, at Douai, that I was for the first time driven to violate corpses before cutting them up. Before then, I had cut up eight or ten dead bodies at Béré, without ever having felt the desire to copulate with them. I have always behaved with them as I had done previously with dead animals: when I had disinterred them, I dismembered them and masturbated before them. It was only after the Douai cemetery incident that the erotic mania began to precede the urge to destroy. But then the latter grew more and more violent with relation to the first, and I experienced much greater pleasure in dismembering bodies after having violated them, than I had felt in merely caressing them. In fact there is no doubt that the destructive impulse has always been more violent in me than the erotic impulse. I believe that at that time I should never have run the risk of digging up a corpse with the sole aim of violating it, if I had not had the intention of cutting it up into pieces. I maintain that the destructive instinct played the principal role there, and no one can prove the contrary. I suppose I am the best judge of what takes place within me. The act of cutting up the corpses was not for one moment destined to conceal the profanation committed, as certain persons have asserted. The urge to dismember the bodies was incomparably more violent in me, than the urge to violate them."

Predisposition to Congenital Pederasty

Similar sexual frenzies may be observed in the last stages of degeneration, in cretinism, in idiots and imbeciles. In the latter there has been noted an unnatural tendency to intercourse with animals.[1] Elsewhere, extreme degrees of degeneration are at times accompanied by absolute brute stupidity, with disappearance of the sex instinct. We see from that, that congenital pederasty, like all other sexual perversions manifested in the field of hereditary infirmities, is not a morbid entity, but merely a symptom, and fortunately, a relatively rare symptom of psychic degeneration. Likewise all conditions which bring about such psychic degeneration may be dependent upon some congenital disorder of the sexual function. Here, the first and most important place is taken by hereditary disposition to nervous affections. A father, who is epileptic, or afflicted with some form or other of cerebral ailment; a mother subject to hysteria, or possessing a pathologic predisposition; in case of atavism, a nervous illness of the grandfather or grandmother, or other parent, these are the causes which, together with other possible hereditary tendencies, are the principal factors in the predisposition to perversion of the sexual instinct.

There follows the predisposition due to the age of the parents, and more particularly to their habits of intemperance. We must note here the fact confirmed by the observations of Flemming, Rurot, Demeaux and oth-

---

1. Mierzejewski: *Forensische Gynäkologie,* p.264.

ers, that children born of parents who are usually sober, but by chance drunk at the time of the procreative act, are psychopaths to the highest degree, and predisposed to nervous disorders and insanity. Syphilis in the parents likewise possesses an influence whose importance cannot be overlooked among the causes contributing to diminution of the reproductive power of the organism. At the present time I know two families where the mother and father were both syphilitic and gave birth to numerous children. The first-born suffered from congenital forms of the disease and were treated for it in their infancy. The others, born during the tertiary, or gummatous stage, showed no visible signs of syphilitic infection during their childhood, but offered a perfect picture of neuropathic constitution in the field of degeneracy.

One of the boys, when he was nine years old, at the sight of prints, paintings or statues representing nude men, would enter a state of excitation terminated by fits of hysteria, after which he was unable to find sleep for several nights. Another, aged eight, when he bathed with older boys, became still more excited, had erections, and pretending to play, would take hold of their genital parts. Each time after these baths, the excitation accompanied by insomnia would last several days. As I have already pointed out, the parents of these two boys were at the time of their conception suffering from syphilis in its late stages, but gave evidence of no hereditary tendency to nervous disease.

Mountainous Cradles of Pederasty

Another cause for the development in children of a neuropathic constitution with sexual perversion may be found in various depressing conditions which may have weighed down upon the parents at the time of fecundation, as for example, if the father or mother was barely recovering from a serious illness like typhoid fever, pneumonia, physical exhaustion, advanced anemia, mental over-fatigue, venereal excess, and so on, in short, anything which might tend to weaken the nervous system and procreative power of the parents.

Lastly, among the active causes which produce psychic degeneration we must include the influence of soil and climate. Among the inhabitants of high mountainous regions such as the Alps, Cordilleras, Himalayas, we very frequently meet with a high degree of sexual perversion, even complete disappearance of the sex instinct, besides cretinism and idiocy.

The Persians affirm that the mountainous portion of Armenia, a high plateau of a six to ten thousand foot elevation, was the original cradle of pederasty. We must compare this with the reports of travelers eminently worthy of credence, reports of the greatest interest. According to them, a prolonged stay at very high altitudes attenuates sexual desire and weakens erections. The latter reappear with new vigor when one goes down to the valleys again. This diminution in sexual desire may in part explain the relatively small growth of population in mountainous regions, and as the cause is hereditary, it constitutes one of the grounds of degeneration which leads to perversion of the sexual instinct.

In the series of phenomena of degeneration, the most frequently observed form of abnormal procreative sense is passive pederasty, with indifference towards women, and accompanied by other relatively unimportant psychic irregularities. The mind and will may be normally developed, and by virtue of this, it is always possible for the morbidly predisposed young boy to be diverted from performing the act of sodomy. His sexual frigidity towards women is congenital, and the inclination towards men is equally so. The latter is sometimes manifested, quite unconsciously at first, by immoderate enthusiasm for the bravery, generosity and intellectual power of men. Later on it is transformed into admiration for masculine beauty, dexterity, vigor, etc. Then comes the ardent desire to see the beloved one, to talk with him, to idolize him. Still later erection and ejaculation are brought on by mere contact with his person. All of this serves to establish the predisposition of pederasty. But the propensity for the act of sodomy is itself never innate.

When the abnormally predisposed young man has, thanks to good education, kept his mind free from contamination and his imagination pure, the act of pederasty, or more accurately that of sodomy, appears to him quite as unclean and disgusting as to the normal individual. A certain depravity, lack of will on the part of the young man, or the influence of example, or continual stimulation, temptation, craft or degree of violence coming from the active party, these are the necessary conditions for arriving at complete performance of the act of pederasty. There is nothing fatal, inevitable or unchangeable in that. For that very good reason it is always possible through judicious guidance to divert the predisposed boy from active sodomy. However, one does not always succeed in overcoming his sexual aversion for women, or his indifference to them.

We have had numerous instances of subjects who were aware of their sexual perversion since childhood. At the same time they recognized the horror and abomination of pederasty, the scorn with which society stigmatizes it; they felt disgust at the abominable act and always refrained from it. In Shaw and Ferris'[1] observation, for example, a man of 35, mentally and physically well developed, through the power of will overcame the desire to embrace a man. The company of men always threw him into a state of erethism, and even during a medical examination he would get an erection. Sometimes he was seized with a violent desire to hug and kiss a man who had pleased him, but always controlled himself despite perpetual terror that a time might come when he would no longer be master of himself. This terror and the wish to liberate himself led him to seek calm through medical treatment.

---

1. J. C. Shaw and N. Ferris: Perverted Sexual Instinct. *Journal of Nervous and Mental Disease*, 1883, no.2.

In the observations of Charcot and Magnan[1] we likewise find the story of a man who from childhood on felt an inclination for men, and who used to become so excited at sight of a virile member, that he would immediately have a spermatic emission. Though quite indifferent towards women, and fully aware of his anomalous condition, in brief, though he knew he was a born pederast, he succeeded by exercise of reason and force of will in abstaining from pederastic practices throughout his life. In this case the skillful treatment selected by Charcot and Magnan gave such brilliant results that at the end of one year the patient was able to have normal relations with women, and even to make plans for marriage.

The sooner the innate defect is perceived, the more judiciously the mind and will are developed, the more practical the means utilized to cause maximum delay and diminution in the appearance of the sex instinct, the more we may hope that the unfortunate young man affected with morbid predisposition will be susceptible to preservation from the horrible vice. We may here call attention to the fact that the subject's aversion for women decreases all the more easily as he learns through force of will to surmount his predilection for men. In several cases of young men afflicted with congenital sexual perversion, we have seen that at 25 or 30 they have become capable of having intercourse with women, of marrying and having children.

---

1. Charcot and Magnan, *loc. cit.*

CHAPTER SIX

Celebrated Affairs and Trials for Criminal Eroticism

To the congenital forms of sexual perversion we must add the morbid deviations of the procreative sense which become manifest at certain times, then completely disappear, and after a certain interval reappear with new violence. These are cases of temporary pederasty, so to speak. Such individuals are periodically subject to an abnormal sexual tendency, and periodically perform the sex act in more or less abnormal fashion. It is not rare for them to be married men, fathers of families, yielding intermittently to pederasty just as dipsomaniacs abandon themselves to their craving for drink.

This periodic type of abnormal sexual satisfaction is very often manifested in the form of active pederasty and flagellation. The patients satisfy their perverted instinct two or three times in the course of a year, and the rest of the time have normal relations with women.

Married Men as Pederasts

The more clearly marked the periodicity of these attacks of sexual perversion, and the more acute the morbid disorder, the more it approaches the form of maniacal excitation with periodic recurrences, that is to say the culminating point of the external manifestations of psychic degeneration.

In fact there are cases known of married men, well-endowed mentally, fathers of families, who from time to time, and sometimes after long intervals, have gone back to pederasty, flagellation or necrophily, or have again experienced an irresistible urge to submit to the coarsest, most indecent treatment, insulting appellations and blows administered by catamites, active pederasts or prostitutes.

As in all forms of periodic mania, during the intervals between attacks the patients have full possession of their mental faculties, and consequently are able to hide their carefully dissembled attacks from even their most intimate friends. For example, one subject spent a very long time in teaching a prostitute how to flagellate him in a special manner, giving her advance notice that at the end of a certain time he would pay her a visit. At this time she would not have to say anything, but must without a word throw him onto the bed and then flog him in accordance with his previous instructions. After some time he did in fact come back to her, silent, gloomy, completely different from his former self, "very queer," as the prostitute said. He undressed, stretched out on the bed, suffered flagellation, during which he mumbled some incoherent words, became highly excited, had an ejaculation, then fell asleep for several hours and went off without a word. After this incident, the attack having passed, he visited the woman, paid her the agreed price, meanwhile calling her attention to the fact that certain of his instructions had not been carried out during his fit. From that time on, he got into the habit of visiting her once every two or three months when seized with his attacks. This went on for several years. He never had normal relations with her, but simply had himself whipped, always in the same way.

Another patient, whose history was communicated to me by my excellent friend, Doctor M. Witz, was in the habit of charging a person, in his employ and informed with his disorder, with making certain extremely complicated preparations before his attacks. A private a- partment was rented beforehand in which a prostitute was installed as housekeeper, with a cook and cham- ber-maid, likewise prostitutes, all three well instructed in what they would have to do. When the attack came on, the patient, who knew no one in the house, would present himself. He was undressed, subjected to var- ious violences to his sexual parts, masturbated, flagel- lated, etc., all in fixed order and according to a care- fully established plan. He would put up a feigned resistance, swore, threw himself into a rage, begged to be left in peace, but in the long run submitted to every- thing. They would then give him food, order him to bed, and would not permit him to leave despite his protestations, and when he refused to obey, they would beat him. This lasted several days. When the attack had passed, as might be detected by certain symptoms known to the trusted employee, who supervised the whole affair without being seen, the patient was allowed to go. At the end of a few days he would return to his home and family who had not the slightest idea of his disorder. He was a rich business man, shrewd and well-informed, and therefore was always able to manage some plausible pretext to explain his absence during the period of his seizure, which came on once or twice a year.

A third patient who adored his beautiful wife, brought up his children admirably, and who was himself of noble, poetic nature, secretly seduced two young boys, brothers, and gradually led them to become alternately active and passive pederasts. Then, several times a year, he would go with them to a room in a bathing establishment and would make them practice pederasty in his presence, a practice in which he too took an active part. The rest of the time he felt no pederastic desires, and was fond of women's company. Yet he defended this particular form of sexual perversion with a certain amount of wit.

We must include in the class of periodic pederasty an episode from the celebrated trial of the "Rue Basse des Remparts," in Paris, in the year 1845, when 47 persons were accused of sodomy and corruption. A woman who rented furnished rooms and was also a procuress deposed that in order to satisfy one of her clients who from time to time visited her and was in the habit of giving her very detailed instructions beforehand, she had dressed up a pederast whom she knew in her own clothes, with bonnet, veil, and blond curly wig, and in this outfit, never varied he would place himself at the disposal of the customer. The latter paid handsomely for this privilege.

We may add to this an observation by Lasègue[1] concerning periodic exhibitionists, young men showing no sign of decrepitude. For example, a rich man aged thirty, of fine appearance, was arraigned before the magistrate, having to answer for offenses against public morality in churches. He was in the habit of entering a church in which there were few people, at the close of day, and there he would spy out some solitary woman in prayer, would approach her, exhibit his genital organs and after a brief moment would withdraw. As he declared to the physician, an irresistible impulse would take possession of him at certain times, and in spite of his resistance, he was forced to follow his fatal leaning and knowingly perform a senseless act.

In other cases known to us the attacks of sexual perversion assumed the form of pederasty practiced concurrently with normal relations with women, or pederasty together with masturbation, etc.

---

1. Lasègue: *Union Médicale*, ler mai, 1877.

Pederastic Drive of Sexually Normal Men

Except at these attacks, all the patients cited above were capable of normal intercourse with women. Most of them were married and did not ask their wives to indulge in any practice outside the normal performance of the sex act. Some suffered terrible pangs of remorse at times, the consciousness of their vice leaving them prey to deep melancholy, for they dreaded the ruin of their domestic happiness, or getting into difficulties with the law. But when the free interval drew near its close, and the seizure approached, the patient became uneasy, lost assurance, and felt an unconquerable desire to perform the sex act in a certain perverted manner. The nearer the moment of the attack, the less able he felt to effect normal coitus. The patient begins to fear that he will be unable to master himself and will betray himself to his wife and friends. As the morbid urge increases, it stifles every other thought and desire, continually haunts the sufferer without a moment's respite, allows him no rest by day or night, depriving him of the capacity for occupying himself with any activity and of the power to concentrate his attention on any other subject. The patient feels that if he must go on struggling, something terrible will happen. He is in dread of losing the freedom of his will and going mad. He gives up, satisfies his morbid diversion, but often, looking back with horror upon what has taken place, he feels contempt for his own weakness and returns to his accustomed way of living and to normal sexual activity.

Precautions for Maintaining Secrecy

Since these periodic pederasts rarely confide their secret to others, their extreme reserve makes them differ from other individuals affected with this perversion. They avoid associating with pederasts, even avoid making friends with young men, are repelled by talk of abnormal sex relations, and above all, manifest none of the outward signs of habitual pederasty. It is only the acute attack, or fear of being discovered, that may lead them to reveal their misery, and in every detail they then disclose, we may read the painful consciousness they have of their weakness and moral letdown. Some of them, in the interval between attacks, look with contempt upon pederasts. Certain ones even give evidence of morbid hatred, particularly for effeminate-looking catamites, in which respect they resemble those dipsomaniacs who during the periods separating their sprees cannot bear wine, or even tolerate the smell of it without feeling disgust.

Yet they know intuitively that at the end of a certain time the morbid tendency will revive, and with new, irresistible power will drive them to commit a whole series of acts whose mere memory during free intervals will inspire them with horror. When the attack is imminent, the fear they experience of not being able to conceal it from their friends by sufficient shrewdness and self-mastery, forces some of them to prepare for the inevitable event during untroubled intervals, and to think up all possible precautions for maintaining the greatest secrecy.

Sudden Unmasking of Debauchees

Where the habitual means the patient resorts to for satisfying his morbid propensity are made impracticable through fortuitous circumstances, or if the attack takes him unawares, he acts under the influence of an irresistible sexual stimulation, and then he either uses violence, or else so little caution that he attracts attention, has himself apprehended by the police, and ruins the happiness of his home. He loses his social standing and in a moment of despair may have recourse to suicide, or to the great surprise of most of his friends, may show up in the prisoners' dock. A man whom everybody considered well-balanced, the respectable father of a family, a talented functionary or a courageous general, is suddenly unmasked and discovered to be the worst of debauchees, who satisfies his sexual passions in the most unnatural, most depraved manner.

Krafft-Ebing[1] mentions one of these cases of periodic sexual perversion involving bestiality, but to my mind the fact requires confirmation. An engineer, aged 45, father of a family, abruptly leaves his business in Trieste, and makes a hasty departure for Vienna in order to join his wife. During the trip he quits the train at an intermediate station, reaches the nearest town, enters a house and there violates an old woman of 70 whom he was seeing for the first time. Arrested immediately afterwards, he declared that so furious a desire for

---

1. Krafft-Ebing, *Arch. f. Psychologie und Nervenkrankheiten*, 1877, Bd. VII, p.296.

copulation had taken possession of him, that he had dashed out of the train to look for a flaying-plant or slaughter-house, in order to satisfy his passion upon one of the many dogs that loiter about such places. But having no success in his quest, and the need becoming so imperious that he could no longer contain himself, he had entered the first house he came to and satisfied his passion upon the first woman encountered. He had already had several similar attacks of sudden rut, and had often satisfied them upon dogs.

The prisoner's mind was sound. He recognized the abominable nature of his act and explained it by a morbid exaggeration of the sex impulse which from time to time dominated him. Since his childhood he had been a neuropath. From 1864 to 1867 he had suffered from recurrent mania with exaggeration of sexual desire. During the last six years he had been perfectly sound in mind.

It is evident that we find here not only a case of exaggerated genital excitation, as Krafft-Ebing says, but a pathologically perverted instinct which fortunately is expressed in a manner not very common. The patient suddenly detecting the premonitory symptoms of the attack, of which he has sad experience, hastily leaves for Vienna, where he may secretly satisfy his passion with animals. But time is pressing, he tries to find a slaughter-house where famished dogs usually wander about. He finds none, and completely beside himself, falls upon the first poor old woman he meets, and immediately violates her.

If it had been a simple case of exaggerated sexual desire, he would at least have been able to satisfy it momentarily by masturbation or by seeking the necessary relief in one of the houses of prostitution in Trieste. He would not have needed then to run off in search of a dog, and would not have violated an old woman in a moment of frenzy, without taking the slightest precaution. It is precisely this instant of frenzy which terrorizes those who suffer periodically from sexual perversion; it is that which leads them to take precautions before the dreaded paroxysm.

In certain particularly pronounced cases, the attack may seize upon the patient unexpectedly. That is what happened to the schoolmaster L . ., who practiced sodomy upon a little two-year-old boy.[1] L . ., twenty-six years old, married and father of a family, gave himself up from time to time to drink. On the 9th of August, slightly drunk, he took the little child from his mother, carried him off on his arm to the garden, placed him on a see-saw and violated him. The mother rushed up on hearing the terrible shrieks uttered by the child, and saw L . . unbuttoned, holding the bloodstained child on his knees. She seized the child and immediately carried him home. L . ., too, disappeared at once. The following day, when interrogated by the

---

1. Mierzejewski, *Forensische Gynäkologie*, p.235.

magistrate, he answered each question by saying "my head burned on all sides". Transported to the hospital the same day, he developed symptoms of cerebral congestion, remained speechless, breathing heavily, sunk in a torpor. He was sick for the next three weeks, with occasional fits of melancholy, and complained of violent headaches. After the initial application of vesicatory, erysipelas supervened, and it was not before the 16th of September that he recovered his senses. Then he declared that he remembered nothing at all of what had happened to him on the 9th of August, and that it could not have been drink, but rather madness which led him to the crime. It was not the first time that his brain had been beclouded this way.

L.. was condemned by the court to penal servitude, but on appealing, the higher court recognized, in accordance with the officially expressed opinion of medical experts, that the incriminating act had been committed under the domination of a mental disorder of morbid origin. L.. died in prison before a final decision was rendered.

Von Gock[1] has published an instance of mental perturbation which had attained an even more decided stage, with maniacal erethism, and periodically increased tendency to pederasty. A 22-year old Jew, of poorly developed intelligence, during his stay in the sanitarium, was in the habit of taking hold of the gen-

---

1. *Archiv. f. Psychologie*, 1875, p.566.

itals of all the employees, and proposing that they engage in pederasty with him. He himself desired to play the passive role. At the end of some time his condition improved and he left the establishment, but a few months later the morbid seizure reappeared with more pronounced tendencies to pederasty.

In these last two cases the symptoms of a constitutional psychopathic state with reduced understanding were clearly established, even aside from the attack of sexual perversion. Such subjects most frequently end up in prison or go straight to the insane asylum. But there are other better-endowed patients, better-developed from the point of view of intelligence, who, once convinced that they have committed such a crime, seek refuge in suicide, like the French general N . ., whose case was in all the newspapers some years ago.

The tendency to necrophily which is observed in rare cases, in the form of isolated attacks separated by long, lucid intervals, must likewise be considered a periodic sexual perversion. It is in fact entirely probable that the case of sexual perversion noted in a church dignitary, and reported by Léo Taxil[1], assumed the periodic character. Here is what the author says: "In a well-known house of prostitution in Paris, according to the patient's own account, there existed a room whose walls were draped with black satin bearing silver teardrops, a funereal decoration. At the sides of the bed

---

1. Léo Taxil: *La Prostitution contemporaine*, p.171.

were placed silver candle-sticks, and on the bed there lay a prostitute completely daubed in white, so as to present the greatest possible resemblance to a corpse. This prostitute had to remain stretched out without making a single motion, her arms crossed upon her breasts. At the hour agreed upon, the prelate would enter in sacerdotal vestments, would kneel before the bed of the pretended corpse, murmur some incoherent words, as if celebrating mass for the dead, then suddenly he would throw himself upon the victim, who as long as this lasted, had to play the part of a corpse and remain lying motionless and speechless."

Brierre de Boismont[1] has reported another example. A girl of 16, of an honorable family, had just died in a small provincial French town. During the night the mother of the young deceased heard the sound of furniture overturned in the room where the dead body lay. She ran in and saw before her an unknown man, divested of all clothing save his undershirt, and who was rising from the bed on which the body rested. She uttered a cry which made several persons run up, and they seized the intruder. The latter seemed to pay no attention to all that was taking place around him and gave completely incoherent answers to all the questions with which they plied him. The examination of the dead body revealed that coitus had been practiced several times upon it.

---

1. *Gazette médicale,* 21 juillet, 1849.

Life Imprisonment for Violation of Corpses

The judicial inquest demonstrated that those who were entrusted with watching over the body had been bribed, that the prisoner was the possessor of a large fortune, had received a good education, frequented the highest society, and that by spending great sums of money and employing all sorts of stratagems, he had often gained access to the bodies of girls just dead, and proceeded to violate them. The court sentenced him to life imprisonment.

Attentive, continued observation of this class of subjects afflicted with periodic sexual perversion makes it perfectly possible to discover in every one of them numerous stigmata of necropathy, of excitable character, or of heavily burdened heredity. On the other hand, superficial, generalized knowledge of these patients makes them appear to have very few points in common with the above described types of congenital pederasts with regard to their outward appearance, manners, style of living, etc.

Recent observations tend to indicate that development of sexual aberrations with periodic recurrences is possible outside the hereditary psychopathic constitution. Anjel[1], for example, describes the following case. A married man of middle age, free from hereditary pathologic transmission, had once suffered a fall in a concert-hall and hit his head against the floor, so seriously as to remain stunned for some time. Afterwards he

---

1. Ueber eigenthümliche Anfälle perverser Sexualerregung. *Archiv. f. Psych.*, vol. XV, H.2.

experienced great oppression and felt a weight in the region of the heart, as well as other troubles. Still later he became subject to a special form of seizure consisting of sleepiness, loss of appetite, irritability and mental depression. When he was in this state, the presence of little girls would cause him particular excitation. Even his own little daughters, aged five and six, awakened desires in him which he could master only with difficulty. The cries of children in an adjoining room would make him have erections. He felt irresistibly drawn towards little girls, and although he was fully aware of the criminal, vicious elements in his desires, he would go about the streets to meet children returning from school, would entice little girls into dark corners, would lift their dresses there and lay bare their sexual parts. The attack would last from 8 to 14 days, then he would regain his senses, troubled with remorse, and resume his habitual mode of living, as well as his normal sexual activity. An interval of peace might set in lasting a year, sometimes fifteen months, and after this the attacks would recur with the same force.

Anjel considers the case he describes above as identical with epileptic fits. He compares the paroxysms of abnormal sexual desire to the psychic counterparts in epilepsy a point which we shall study later. I shall simply note here that this explanation does not appear quite conclusive to me for it is well known that the distinctive sign of epileptic psychoses consists in a certain obnubilation of consciousness during the attack. This was lacking in the case just related. Psychic epilepsy is manifested either in a quite sudden manner or by very fleeting precursory signs in the form of "aura". It disappears with equal rapidity, and this, too, was not the case with the subject mentioned above, since the paroxysm was for several days preceded by morbid irritability and moral depression.

Moreover, though memory of the attack may sometimes subsist immediately afterwards, it disappears in the end, and this, too, did not occur in the case reported by Anjel. The absence of any sort of morbid manifestation between paroxysms, as well as the absence of so-called epileptic symptoms and obnubilation of consciousness immediately after the fit, all these facts, I say, authorize my classing Anjel's observation with cases of periodic mania, in the group I designated as periodic perversion of the sexual instinct. The principal interest of the above case is the absence of hereditary neuropathic predisposition. If this fact is accurate, (it is not completely certified in the clinical description) the case would constitute an exception, for in all similar cases of this category the influence of heredity is clearly displayed.

CHAPTER SEVEN

Analyses of Legal Psychiatry in Russia

As epilepsy is one of the most clearly marked forms of psychic degeneration, we may readily conceive from the very outset, that it must often be manifested conjointly with perversion of the sex instinct. From day to day now, it becomes more evident that we are far from having completed the special study of epileptic seizures, those complicated phenomena comprised under the name "epilepsy". In the intervals separating attacks, and after them we can observe a whole series of supplementary phenomena which denote a general affection of the nervous system and a profoundly neuropathic constitution. There has in fact been described a particular pathologic character designated as the "epileptic character".

These are the principal traits in the unamiable character of the epileptic: he is gloomy, excessively irritable at times, shifting without cause from intense activity

to apathy and mental depression; he is cruel and piti-
less, as well as vindictive and hypocritical. All this reveals the existence of a generalized, deep-seated lesion
of the nervous centers.

We can understand at once that sexual perversion and
epilepsy may be frequently in the same subject, since
they both have as common origin some hereditary
taint, and in a general way are the products of the
same etiologic factors behind psychic degeneration.
We may state without exaggeration that hereditary epilepsy is very often encountered in combination with
abnormal sexual instincts. Frequently it happens that
the sexual potency of the epileptic is much reduced;
coitus can be effected only with difficulty and is little
sought after. Sometimes epileptics do not satisfy their
sex desires with women, but abandon themselves at an
early age to masturbation. When the period of virility
arrives, the erethism is at times so amplified that ejaculation follows immediately after erection, whence the
impossibility of normal coition with women. These
masturbating epileptics may very well be ranged right
after pederastic epileptics, generally active. Besides,
all the previously described forms of hereditary sexual perversion may be encountered concurrently with
epilepsy.

In such cases epilepsy is but one of the symptoms indicative of grave psychic degeneration, and the manner in which the sexual perversion is expressed no
longer presents distinctive characteristics. Neverthe-

less, there are rare cases of epilepsy in which they have observed peculiar forms of sexual perversion whose significance is tantamount to epileptic psychoses. It is well known that at times epileptics, instead of undergoing a real fit, are subject to sudden mental disturbances, short-lived and quickly produced. These disorders are accompanied by obnubilation of consciousness, delirious hallucinations with ideas of persecution, mysticism or megalomania. In the course of such an epileptoid seizure with loss of perception there may supervene a sexual erethism with imperious desire for gratification. The patient may commit a series of abominable acts, sometimes has abnormal sex relations, and when the attack is over has only a confused recollection of what has happened and can in no way explain his irrational doings.

Some years ago I had occasion to observe a very interesting case which escaped becoming the subject for judicial inquest, thanks to the benevolence of the interested parties. A rich young man of 26 had for about a year been living with a young woman whom he seemed to love very much. During this lapse of time he had had two nocturnal fits of epilepsy following immoderate use of alcoholic liquors. He led a very irregular life, but practiced coitus only rarely, and then in a normal way with the same woman. He displayed no tendency to sexual perversion. One evening, after a dinner during which he had drunk too much wine, he came on foot to his mistress' house and exchanged a few words with the maid who opened the door for him with the information that his mistress had not yet come home. He then made his way with sure steps to the bed-room, from there into an adjoining room where a boy of 14 was sleeping and proceeded to violate him. The lacerated child, wounded in one hand, cried out for help and the maid rushed in, whereupon the patient released the young boy threw himself upon the maid and raped her. He then got into bed without undressing and slept soundly for twelve hours. When he awoke, he at first recalled nothing of what had taken place. A few hours later he remembered having drunk too freely the day before and having had intercourse with a woman. The episode with the young boy had completely gone out of his memory. I saw the patient two days later. He did not want to answer questions, was mentally depressed and attributed everything to his inebriety. Some weeks afterward, he again had epileptic fits, but as far as I could ascertain there was no sexual perversion noted this time.

Dr. Erlicki has kindly communicated to me the case of another epileptic whose attacks were accompanied by exasperation of sexual desire and loss of consciousness. Mr. X . . left college after brilliant studies. For a year or two he led a dissipated life and suffered a few epileptic fits. Then he made a trip to his estate and solicited the hand of a young woman of good family. They agree that the wedding will take place at the home of the girl's parents. All the assembled guests await the arrival of the future husband. The latter makes his appearance accompanied by his brother, walks straight across the room filled with the throng of invited persons, approaches his betrothed, and there unbuttons his trousers and begins to masturbate in view of everybody. He was immediately carried home and taken by his brother to a hospital for mental disorders. Throughout the trip the patient displayed an unconquerable urge to satisfy his desires by masturbating. They noticed the same tendency during the first days after his admission to the clinic, but with decreasing force. When the paroxysm was past, the patient had but a vague, incomplete recollection of what had happened, a large part of it having become entirely obliterated from his memory. He could give no explanation whatever for his acts.

Dr. Kowalewski of Kharkov has communicated a personal observation of a case of associated epilepsy, in which epileptic convulsions were manifested during an attack of maniacal agitation. Once the convulsions had ceased, the maniacal excitation did not persist either. Mr. B . ., forty years of age, previously in good health, became depressed on a certain day, ate nothing and the following morning, in the presence of his wife and three children, began to importune Mrs. B . . (a friend of the family who was seated in the parlor) with the object of having her perform coitus with him. Repulsed by her, he then begged his wife, and heedless of the presence of their friend and the children, implored her to grant him immediate gratification for his desire. As she too refused, he fell to the ground, began to moan, became quite pale and had a furious attack of mania. His wife and the friend having fled from the room, he broke the windows, threw boiling water on all those who came near him, and finally flung their little three-year-old child into the stove. He was acquitted by the court on the ground of irresponsibility. Two and a half years later he entered the district asylum of Dr. Kowalewski being afflicted with highly accentuated epileptic seizures.[1]

The acts of many individuals accused of rape and deeds of sexual perversion may be ascribed to epileptic obnubilation of consciousness with exacerbation of the sex instinct and impulsive actions. Unfortunately this form of transitory mental disorder has been but little studied up to the present time.

Great commotion was produced in Russia a short time ago because of a merchant who, after having committed all sorts of excesses in a house of prostitution in Moscow, recovered his senses in Kiev, 490 miles distant, without having the slightest idea of how and why he had arrived in that place, where he found himself without a penny in his pocket. The judicial investigator was solely concerned with the fact that he had been robbed and paid no attention at all to his state of amnesia. This case recalls the one cited by Legrand du

---

1. Kowalewski, *Analyses of Legal Psychiatry.* (In Russian) 1881, p.61.

Saulle[1] about a French merchant whose traveling companions had been struck by his strange behavior, and who to his great surprise and terror, found himself one day in Bombay, instead of being in Paris.

The peculiarities which distinguish sexual perversion of epileptic origin from the aforementioned forms of periodically abnormal sex instincts are principally these: lack of reflection, neglect of precautions, the absence of any thought of avoiding responsibility for the criminal acts, the intense obnubilation of self-consciousness during their performance, and jumbled memory of what occurred.

---

1. Legrand du Saulle, *Etude médico-légale,* p. 110.

CHAPTER EIGHT

Erotomania and Ecstatic Pederastomania

Now there remains for discussion a psychic state often alluded to by the public, but generally with the most erroneous ideas about the nature of the affection. *Erotomania,* or excitation of the psychic functions in the particular direction of erotic tendencies, may be manifested spontaneously in neuropathic subjects, or as symptom of a much more distinctly marked seizure of psychosis or neurosis. One of the manifestations of psychic degeneration is a morbid disposition for becoming amorous, and this is the outstanding sign of the mental state we are studying. We most frequently encounter it in women, notably in hysterical ones. It is also found in men of clearly neuropathic constitution, who have been addicted to masturbation or suffer a decline in sexual potency. Serious cerebral ailments at a previous time, as in youth, combined with hereditary influences, may also favor development of this condition at times.

The young man who seems unhealthily shy and timid in the company of women may give free reign to his imagination when alone, and generally resorts to masturbation. If the erethism is still greater, and the nervous system is both excitable and debilitated, imagination alone may suffice to bring about seminal emission. When a frequently repeated influence has produced an attachment in the patient for an object or definite person, who becomes the subject of his dream of love, if circumstances continue to be favorable, the initial stage of this erotomania is not long in taking on a much more pronounced form. The patient then idolizes the object of his affection, adores her, sacrifices everything for her, writes to her, composes verses in her honor and becomes unbearable to all those around him by his incessant talk about his love, his sufferings and his ecstasy.

All observers have noted that despite their passion the love of such subjects remains purely platonic. However, absolute platonism seems doubtful in several erotomaniacs I have been able to observe, at least in their beginnings. Many erotomaniacs are incapable of effecting normal coitus, as is the case with most inveterate masturbators having some hereditary taint. A very frequent cause of suicide among them is precisely this impossibility they feel of ever being able to satisfy their ardor with the object of their passion. I have often had occasion to send young men of this type to specialists in neuropathology. They would threaten to commit suicide if they failed to get an immediate cure for their infirmity. They complained of having only incomplete erections and that ejaculation was brought on by mere sight of the beloved person, whereas they found themselves incapable of having normal intercourse with this idol, whose possession alone could save their life from seeming useless. It was not rare for the said idol to be just a common prostitute in a public house who was thinking only of her own gain in her relations with them, or else some married woman who had never given the young lunatics the slightest ground for believing that she was tempted to grant them any intimacies.

Love in patients suffering this way is naturally platonic when its object is a person met by chance, or who occupies a very high rank, some celebrity, etc. But there again masturbation generally provides satisfaction for their overexcited imagination. In proportion as the morbid predisposition progresses, it imperceptibly becomes a real disease. The sick man imagines that the looks and gestures of the object of his passion have a peculiar significance which expresses reciprocity for his feelings or encouragement to persevere in them. As they constantly stimulate their imagination and secretly satisfy themselves by onanism, they often come to have real illusions and hallucinations. Maniacal love may likewise be complicated with ambitious ideas, or again morbid fear of persecution may supervene, alternating with terror and hypochondriasis.

Congential catamites who have been brought up amongst women, far from the depraving influence of pederasts, but without anyone's taking adequate care of their education, easily become erotomaniacs. In such a case the object of their passion is naturally either some hero whose picture they have often had the opportunity of seeing, or some celebrity in music, song or science. The same exaggerated tendency to become amorous, but this time with perverted sex instincts, is manifested in this pathologic state, which we cannot better designate than by the name "pederastomania". Day and night the patient has before his eyes the object of his adoration, whose perfections fill him with ecstasy. These perfections are sometimes imaginary and always exaggerated, and it is to them that he vows eternal reverence and devotion, promises disinterested affection, etc. Every word, every movement of the adored being arouses extraordinary joy and exaltation in our patient, or plunges him into despair, depriving him of appetite and sleep. The general excitation may even grow to the point where it ends in a real fever, which Gorry has described under the name of *fièvre érotique* (erotic fever), or else it may be manifested in the form of a regular attack of mania, with benumbing of consciousness and erotic delirium, the latter being commonly based upon religious or demoniacal ideas.

We always find in the diaries and memoirs of the great majority of catamites the same descriptions of sadness and joy, of hope and fear which characterize the correspondence and autobiographies of hysterical girls and women-erotomaniacs. In subjects with deeply developed erotomania the object of adoration is not always a living being, and this peculiarity may lead to a special aberration of the sex instinct. It is certainly well known that pictures often suffice to excite onanists. In the same way a painting, and especially a statue, may become the erotomaniac's object of adoration.

Ancient Greece is rich in examples of the adoration of statues and records of the efforts made by unhappy erotomaniacs to perform the sex act with them. There is the notorious story of Clysophus who fell in love with a marble statue in the temple of Samos. He hid in the temple and tried to go through the act with it, but could not manage because of the coldness of the marble. Then he made use of a piece of raw meat applied to a particular part of the statue, and by this procedure succeeded in his aims. Another Greek who had become enamored of the statue of Cupid in the temple of Delphi practiced pederasty with it and in gratitude placed at its feet a wreath of great value. The oracle consulted in regard to this, ordered that the madman be set at liberty, for after all he had paid a very high price for a very limited pleasure.

But in our own time, too, statues and pictures have

been the object of adoration by psychopaths. In 1887 French newspapers related the case of a gardener who had fallen in love with a reproduction of the Venus de Milo, set out in a park. And some years ago, in the vicinity of Saint Petersburg they arrested a young man who was in the habit of making moonlight visits to the statue of a nymph situated on the terrace of a country house.

It does not fall within the scope of our work to describe the rare and exceptional cases of sexual perversion which we have ourselves been able to observe, for example those of lunatics and particularly of maniacs who imagine themselves to be women and consequently seek the society of men, as Dr. Raggi has recently reported.[1]

Neither is it our concern to recall cases of sexual mania which we at times encounter together with acts of sudden impulsion, or which appear in the course of various forms of common mania, alcoholic[2], automatic, etc.

We must note that so far as our personal observations have given proof, alcoholism by itself never leads to sexual perversion in subjects of normal constitution. Although in many cases alcohol may have the effect of an excitant, augmenting venereal desires and prolong-

---

1. Raggi, *Aberrazione del sentimento sessuale in un maniaco ginecomasta.* La Salute, 1882, no. 11, p.86.

2. F. D. Crothers, *Inebriate Automatism.* Journal of Nervous and Mental Diseases, no. 2.

ing the duration of the sex act, so far as I have been able to observe it does not tend in normally constituted subjects to produce deviation from the ordinary way of consummating the sex-urge. But on the contrary, in psychopathic subjects predisposed to sexual perversion, and whose predisposition can only be repressed and attenuated by reason, power of will and force of habit, in such subjects the congenital tendency is magnified by drink because of the decrease in self-control and the intensification of sexual desires. The result is that the drunken individual performs a series of acts which he could have refrained from committing when in sober condition.

I knew a doctor of neuropathic constitution who generally had normal relations with women. But as soon as he had drunk some wine, which took quick effect upon him, normal coitus no longer sufficed to satisfy the intensification of his sexual desires. Under these conditions he felt driven to prick a woman's buttocks, or cut them with a lancet. He had to see the blood flow or the blade plunged into the living flesh to experience complete satisfaction through ejaculation.

I may state that several present-day authors, like Moreau de Tours, use the name *satyriasis* to describe a particular neurosis characterized by great magnification of sex desire, a continual state of erection, frequent seminal emissions and an insatiable, morbid need for coition. During this time the other senses are obnubilated. The patient has hallucinations, delirium, furious mania, becomes violent, etc. In short, his self-control is much diminished, and he becomes irresponsible. The development of satyriasis is principally attributed to sexual abstinence, especially under the influence of religious convictions. This fact, for example, is analyzed in the confessions of the Abbé de Cours written by himself and published by Buffon. After a long period of struggle, fasting and prayer, all women began to appear to him as surrounded by a halo of light. Their countenance had a terrible effect upon him. It seemed to him that the king was offering him all the ladies of the court, so that he might break his vows of chastity, etc.[1]

The visions that haunted Saint Anthony far surpassed the ones reported in the above confession.

When patients in this state meet with opposition they may resort to violence, and even commit murder. Léger who was executed in 1834 for raping and murdering a young girl had until that time practiced absolute continence under the influence of religious convictions fortified by the local priest. In such a case where violent mania breaks out, it is easy to understand how an act of pederasty may become possible, even when there is a certain amount of struggle and resistance.

In my opinion we must not consider satyriasis as a distinct psychosis. It is more correct to regard it as a symptom of abnormally intensified excitation of the

---

1. Buffon, *Histoire naturelle de l'homme,* Puberté.

cerebral processes and as a generalized acceleration of
psychic phenomena, which is of regular occurrence in
the maniacal state. Sexual delirium is an accidental
symptom which shows up in many cerebral affections,
and there is no necessity for taking it as a special form
of sexual mania, as is done by Moreau de Tours. This
delirium may appear in all the forms we have described of abnormal sexual instincts, above all where
there is an hereditary taint.

Nor do we consider as cases of satyriasis those morbid
affections which are due to ingestion of cantharides
and other substances called *pocula amatoria* (aphrodisiacs). I have often had occasion to see such patients. The continual erection is at first accompanied
by voluptuous sensations and ejaculation, superseded
by absolute sexual apathy. Later on, erections are followed by hematuria, fever, etc. The phenomena resulting from intoxication by cantharides might even be
designated under the name of *acute priapism*. There,
too, as we shall see later, we find pathologically con-
tinuous erection and absence of voluptuous sensation.

CHAPTER NINE

Pederasty Among Boys--
Preventions

WHEN a child whose sex instinct is perverted enters a large school, especially a boarding-school, comes into contact with many other boys of various ages, whose number makes it difficult to watch over the appearance of puberty and insure its regular development, this child generally becomes a source of contamination for a large part of his comrades. First, there is the violent excitation, at times reaching morbid intensification, which develops as the young boy grows up and remains unsatisfied. Then again there is the tendency to kiss and cajole, to sleep two together in the same bed, and these make possible the first attempts at sexual inter-course. We may add here the influence of common practice and the spirit of imitation.

The big boy, vigorous and active, is always the model for the weaker, younger ones. Through the influence of example, the desire not to lag behind, to show off their boldness, the unfortunate youngsters overcome their repugnance for the unclean act, inflame their imagination with images of women and thus end up in pederasty. The more frequently these abnormal acts are practiced, the more normal, healthy activity of the sex instinct becomes blunted and modified by force of acquired habit. In the beginning the boys required an effort of their enkindled imaginations, with visions of feminine bodies, before they could be sexually excited and led to consider the actual practice of pederasty as an unique, if unpleasant, means of relieving their exacerbated erethism. But with time, disgust gradually wears away, the reality little by little supplants the fantasy and the boy no longer resorts to the latter to provoke the accustomed excitation. In his dreams, as well as in the waking state, sexual excitation becomes associated through usage with the image of the passive pederast. Woman's image, on the contrary, loses its brightness, and the representation of feminine beauty is eclipsed.

For these subjects there is more pleasure with a woman who affects masculine manners, who has her hair cut short, very small breasts, and a narrow pelvis. When the vicious habit has become more and more firmly anchored in the young man, women conclude by no longer being able to excite him at all. The active pederast (*pedicator*) becomes absolutely impotent with women, or at any rate loses the capacity for regular performance of coitus.

Once the force of example, habit or certain restrictions has developed such morbid types, vice becomes installed as master of the house. The tradition is handed down to new-comers by those who graduate. Young boys of effeminate appearance, especially when they first arrive, are subjected to a whole series of temptations for their moral ruination. Sometimes threats and actual maltreatments are used in order to lead them to become passive pederasts. Leading an inexperienced youngster astray and perverting him appear as a sort of meritorious deed which is applauded by the pupils who have left the school. These continue to keep in touch with the institution, sometimes visit it, and during vacations invite some of the students to come to their homes, where their instruction in a special direction is finished off. The school has thus to a certain extent become the center of a group of pederasts. They continue to fetch new victims there and guide them along the vilest paths of vice and moral turpitude. When the young boy is sexually lost, he learns gradually to solicit and receive bounties and gifts from his tutors. He sells his charms and thus comes to be the most contemptible representative of this low vice: "a venal, passive pederast".

Here is his portrait: accustomed to masturbating since childhood; wont to suppress shame and conscience when it pays; disgusted perhaps by unnatural sex relations, but ready, when there is money in it, to stifle his repugnance for the unclean act (as well as for the

person of his purchaser on whom he lavishes smiles
and caresses in return for the most revolting acts that
may be practiced upon man) ; trained from youth to
lying both in word and action, yet looking upon this as
an expression of feeling in keeping with his profession.
He combines in himself all the repugnant traits of the
onanist. Such a creature is equally venal outside the
sexual sphere. He is capable of the most unscrupulous,
most infamous doings. That is why for a long time society has recognized the depravity of such individuals
and stigmatized these prostituted pederasts with the
scorn they deserve.

Pederasty somehow introduced into an educational
institution thus causes a whole series of morbid disorders, not only from the sexual point of view, but also
with regard to morality in general. On one side we find
the active pederast who gradually loses the capacity
for having normal intercourse, who entirely of his own
volition disguises his nature and condemns himself to
the worst privation in life, not only by renouncing the
love of women, but by exposing himself to becoming
the object of their profound contempt, horror and disgust. Though conscious of his vice, he no longer has
the power to give it up. In a fit of despair he may be
ready to destroy his own life, or drown his conscience
in wine and wild orgies in the company of individuals
morally weak, like himself. On the other side stands
the degraded catamite, a venal liar, whose soul is depraved to the very bottom, and who is diseased physi-

cally and morally. And between these two sharply defined types is placed a whole series of perverters and perverted, a complete system of gradual induction into vice, marked by venality and absence of all decency.

Besides the boarding-schools alluded to above, sailing vessels on long trips, prisons, army barracks with schools for soldiers' sons, etc., furnish favorable conditions for the spread and development of acquired pederasty. But as we have already seen, once it has found a peaceful habitat, the concomitance of several other factors is required for pederasty to be propagated with all its consequences. When these factors are lacking, it soon disappears as an isolated, accidental phenomenon.

The intensity of the sex urge varies greatly with the health of the subject. From the time of puberty and then throughout life, the need for sexual gratification is eminently subject to variation, from the point of view of intensity, duration and frequency, as well as in regard to the manner of expression. This results from a combination of causes which there is no room to discuss here. It is important to note, however, that not only persons of quite normal constitution, but also different races may show great variations in intensity of sexual ardor. For persons of sensual temperament, the sexual function constitutes the *primum movens* of existence during a certain period of their life. They sacrifice everything to satisfy their sexual appetite which diminishes all other desires. Such subjects gen-

erally spare themselves no trials, are very enterpriz-
ing and do not have too many scruples about the means
to use for attaining their goal. Their efforts are sometimes crowned with success in spite of obstacles. When
for some cause or other they are unable to obtain normal gratification, the intensity of their desire may
make them resort to masturbation, or in much rarer
instances, they may become active pederasts. They
then choose the most effeminate-looking catamite they
can find, keep strictly to sodomy, and at the first favorable opportunity pederasty is replaced by intercourse
with women. These subjects are, so to speak, occasional pederasts.

However, when such an individual who has spent the
larger part of his life in having continual relations
with women and who has never felt any interest whatever outside the regular sex functions, comes to realize that from long-continued excesses, coitus too-often
repeated or other causes, his sexual potency has begun
to wane (though desire still persists with all its pris-
tine vigor) he then has recourse to various stimulatory
measures. After having tried all other means, after
having inflamed his imagination and so aroused his
senses still more, and as the procreative power contin-
ues to decline from day to day, he sometimes applies
to passive pederasty as an excitant which will favor
erection and thus facilitate sexual gratification. In such
cases pederasty is not an end, but simply one of many
means of excitation. The latter are often combined in

a particular systematic order which has come to be an absolute necessity for a man accustomed to make coition the predominant business of his life, and who feels himself growing more impotent daily.

Disorder may likewise exist in ordinary sexual temperaments where the ardor is relatively feeble. The development of strength of character, of the power of mastering one's passions and repressing them has great importance in this connection. In sensitive natures, desire as a general rule takes on rapid, high intensity and then determines certain activities or provokes new desires. Otherwise such individuals follow the teachings of common sense, morality, habit, and the sense of duty.

When the power of resistance in its various aspects has been insufficiently cultivated by education, sensitivity inasmuch as it favors quick awakening of desire, also demands its immediate gratification. In the sexual order this ends in incontinence. That is why a subject sexually weak may commit excesses. The slightest carnal desire arouses in him an imperious, irresistible drive to seek gratification, and a weak subject having a tendency to sexual insufficiency may thus reach exhaustion, or a stage where excitation is of decreased intensity and erection incomplete. The mildest stimulation is enough to cause such an inidividual to abandon himself to the sex urge. The latter grows rapidly in consequence of the hypersensitivity and irritable debility of the nervous system, and the patient considers it so great that in the long run the capacity for satisfying it falls far below his expectations. Physical lassitude and satiety set in before psychic satisfaction. The harmony and perfect gradation which characterize the normal sex act are lacking. Complete gratification becomes a matter of chance, and the patient, who gradually loses his procreative power while striving to bring about excitation, seeks to discover new means or finds them with individuals having morbid affections and afflicted with a perverted sex instinct. In this case imitation becomes one of the most powerful agents for propagating perversity.

We have a model in the realm of fashions, where a style may begin with some eminent personage or privleged class of society, and then becomes the general tendency, the current mode.

The weaker the development of the faculty for receiving impressions, for assimilating and transforming them into new productions of the mind, for reproducing them through the force of imagination, and in general, the weaker the creative power, taken in its broadest sense, then the stronger is the tendency to imitation. And just as in all matters of style a propensity for imitation is the index of a lack of independence, of an insufficient stability of ideas, so in the sphere of sexual activities the urge to imitate gives rise to a whole series of senseless acts, the latter being provoked by excitations having no relation whatever to the sex act. The desire to ape a certain person, at least to equal him in depravity, or if possible to surpass him, the thirst for creating a sensation or astounding by some extraordinary action, these are some of the factors which make many mean, superficial, mentally inferior characters fall into the habit of abnormal forms of sex practices, without their being at all incited by a natural need on their part. The proof of this is in the rapid diffusion of various sexual aberrations which as symptoms of disease are but rarely encountered.

There are for example observations of patients stricken with senile dementia for whom the sight of a woman in the act of defecating brings on an erection. Some years ago in Paris a certain number of men of high position were afflicted with this morbid perversion. At the present time, according to L. Taxil[1], "stercoraires", as they are called, are no longer an exceptional phenomenon. In houses of prostitution there are special arrangements prepared towards this end, and healthy young men, in spirit of imitation, repeat the morbid acts of certain weak-minded persons renowned for a while because of their dissolute life.

It must be noted that under these conditions pederasty and flagellation as excitants are propagated especially by favor of certain books written by persons affected with congenital perversion of the sex instinct. Such is the case with the celebrated Marquis de Sade, author of "La nouvelle Justine, ou les malheurs de la ver-

---

1. L. Taxil, *loc. cit.*, p. 166.

tu". He was a congenital pederast sentenced to prison several times, and even condemned to death for outrages against decency and for murder. At the end of his life, he fell into senile dementia and died in 1814, in the insane asylum at Charenton. He had been incarcerated there for cruel tortures inflicted upon a woman. This psychopathic author puts his own morbidly abnormal sensations into the mouth of his hero, and makes an ardent plea for sodomy. In the images and descriptions which shock by their cynicism and the sexual perversion revealed, the debauchee grown feeble seeks to discover new stimulants, and follows the counsels of a monomaniac.

It is the same with flagellation. Le Riche de la Popelinière[1] describes the manifestations of his own sex impulse and congenital perversion in the form of a series of disconnected dialogues rather poor in style and substance. He attributes to flagellation such a stimulatory power as could have been born only of the diseased fancies of a madman's brain. Nevertheless, when his sexual potency is on the wane, it is to these stimuli that the debauchee hastens to have recourse.

---

1. *Tableaux des moeurs du temps dans les différents âges de la vie.* Avec note de Charles Monselet, Paris, 1867.

CHAPTER TEN

Pederasty in the Orient

PEDERASTY, too, comes up again in the acquired form of sexual perversion, and prevails so to speak in endemic state amongst several Oriental peoples. It is correct, however, to say that pederasty is far from being as common and customary in the Orient as is often maintained. It is forbidden there by religion, and to a certain extent prosecuted by the laws. Nevertheless it finds a more favorable soil for cultivation in the Orient than in Europe. The absolute exclusion of women from social life, their sequestration, the impossibility of their having any sexual intercourse whatever outside of marriage, and often even the necessity for permission by the parents, and the payment of an adequate sum of money by the intended husband to secure delivery of his bride, all these conditions put young Moslems in the position of pupils at a boarding-school.

Open Display of Pederasty in Orient

What tends further to develop the senile form of pederasty is premature indulgence in sexual pleasures and the abuse of coitus in rich families which leads to satiation of the senses. Similarly, great disparity in age between an old man and a young woman who serves as his slave is a powerful provocative agent for degeneration in the offspring, and consequently of sexual perversion.

The numerous passive pederasts met with especially in rich families where this vice possesses an hereditary foothold, serve not only to gratify perverted sex instincts. The fortune and importance of a Mussulman are at times measured by the number of young men he keeps in his service, expensively attired in special style. One may often see a whole troop of these maintained out of vanity by persons to whom pederasty is absolutely repugnant. Pederasty is more openly displayed in the Orient, much less dissimulated, and frequently rich depraved men are known to take pride in possessing a beautiful boy, just as among us, men are proud to have a costly mistress.

Setting this aside, we see that the intellectual pursuits of life are more limited in the Orient, often specially directed towards sexuality. There follows from that a development of depravity in its basest form, and we have observed that this may end up in acquired pederasty. Since this abnormal manner of sex-gratification is so pathological a phenomenon and so contrary to nature, since it is so much opposed to the organism and so harmful to the propagation of the species, it would certainly be a mistake to admit that in the Orient or anywhere else it could be recognized as normal, regular and lawful. Pederasty, like every other hideous deformity, provokes horror in the mind of the normally developed man always and everywhere, while in the mind of woman it arouses disgust and contempt.

CHAPTER ELEVEN

Pederasty in Old Men: Perils-- Horrors of Marshal Gilles de Rais

WE often find a variety of aberrations in the course of senile dementia. But this denomination does not precisely correspond with the main condition under consideration, for the phenomena described are not exclusively encountered in old men, and are far from being accompanied at all times by failure of mind.

Complete pathological types of senile dementia are observed especially after the age of sixty, but preliminary symptoms may be manifested much earlier. The sooner the individual has exhausted his energy and vitality, whether in excessive struggle for existence, in early abandonment to wild passions, or in efforts made to overcome serious maladies, the sooner does the morbid state appear, and the more rapidly it develops. A peacefully conducted life, on the contrary, will present no morbid manifestations in old age. It may therefore be quite unexceptional to encounter senile dementia in

101

middle-aged subjects, whereas we may find men of advanced years who possess very youthful freshness of mind and feelings.

The disease itself consists principally in a diminution of cerebral nutrition with consecutive atrophy of the nervous components. At the same time there is alteration in the vascular walls and blood system of the brain, and consequent shrinkage, dilation, thrombosis or rupture of the vessels,etc. While these modifications of the regular blood circulation in the brain are being produced they give rise to a whole series of successive morbid phases which, in addition to thickening or thinning of the skull bones, bring on localized softening of the brain matter, together with degradation and pathologic enfeeblement of mental power. Since the morbid state in question constitutes but a part of the general decay of the whole organism and coincides with a functional decline in the entire nutritional sphere, it finds its final expression in senile decrepitude.

This gradual degeneration of the organism in all its organs and systems is not produced equally throughout, and may be manifested in quite different ways. In some cases the predominant symptom may be physical debility coincident with perfect soundness of the mental faculties. In others, there are primary organic modifications in the brain evinced by changes in character and intelligence, while the physical powers remain intact. In the latter order of things the outstanding trait is often a deviation of the sexual sense which may be revealed in a multitude of different manners. The earliest symptom common to all such cases is an increasing indecency of language, particularly in conversations with young persons, even little boys. Patients of this sort have a special fondness for demoralizing youngsters and depraving them, by means of exciting pictures, obscene books and tales. In this way they begin by leading them to masturbate, then little by little to practice passive pederasty.

In other cases, sexual perversion takes a different direction under the influence of the hemorrhoidal accidents and prurigo which so commonly accompany old age. The patient himself then becomes a passive pederast and lets his victims play the active role. Quite often the afflicted individual alternates as passive and active pederast, or may strive to perform the act of sodomy upon little girls, four or five years old.

Though these individuals are at first extremely cautious, suspicious and reserved, in proportion as they lose their intelligence, strength of will and especially their memory and judgment, they lose the power of self-mastery. They permit their abnormal condition to appear more clearly and may perpetrate acts of criminal brutality upon young men and children, pushing their shamelessness to the farthest extremes. Because of the steady augmentation of their moral and physical decay, this indecency may at moments take on a quite naive form, while at other times it is altogether disgusting and dirty. A feeble-minded old man will for instance entice little children to his home and will show them his genital organ, long incapable of erection and ejaculation.

A whole set of these patients has been described by Lasègue[1] under the name of exhibitionists. In one case a man of 60, holding a high position in the government, used to exhibit his sexual parts to a little girl aged 8 who lived across the way from him. Then again, there was a general leading a very regular life, of superior mind and education, who was in the habit of stopping in front of the gate of a house where some little girls were living. He would expose his parts before them for a few minutes and then silently withdraw. An old writer, aged 65, whose life was quiet and respectable, was arrested by the police for public outrages against decency. He used to exhibit himself to women who passed by in the street. All the patients cited here had full possession of their mental faculties at the beginning of their disorder, but subsequent observations gave evidence of numerous pathologic deviations in the sphere of the central nervous system. Towards the end of their lives undeniable symptoms of senile dementia did indeed make their appearance.

There are other cases where satisfaction of the sex desire is accompanied by the most incredible and most disgusting acts. The subject will have a woman defe-

---

1. Lasègue, *Les Exhibitionistes*, Union médicale, ler mai 1877.

cate into his mouth, or will himself defecate on the
naked body of a woman. I knew one such patient who
was in the habit of making a woman dressed in a very
low-cut ballet-dancer's costume lie down on a divan in
a brilliantly lighted drawing-room. He would gaze at
her for some time, then once the erection had set in,
he would fling himself upon her and void his feces onto her bosom. During this time he would have a sort
of ejaculation. We might range this case in the class of
periodic sexual perversion, if there had not been concurrently a pronounced and growing tendency on the
patient's part towards passive pederasty, together with
other mental manifestations which clearly denoted the
inception of senile dementia.

Still more astounding and disgusting are the aberrations of those who are called in French "renifleurs"
(sniffers). Tardieu has had to borrow Latin to describe
them. "Foedissimum tandem et singulare genus libid-
inosorum vivido colore exprimit appellatio" renifleurs,
"qui in secretos locos nimirum circa theatrorum post-
icos convenientes quo complures feminae ad mictur-
iendum festinant, per nares urinali odore excitati, il-
lico se invicem pollunt".[1]

Cases where the sex act is performed with fowls, like
hens and geese, must also be classed under the head
of senile perversion. The state of morbid overexcite-
ment reaches its climax at sight of the dying animal,

---

1. Tardieu, *Etude médico-légale sur les attentats aux moeurs*, p.206.

and its last convulsions procure an extreme sensual satisfaction for the patient at the time of coitus.

Restless, irritable, sleepless, the patient, whose mind is going under from day to day, falls into a second childhood. Causeless gaiety and laughter alternate with tears and ill humor. The sexual sense is at times expressed in the most cruel manner. The old man suffering this way will fondle a child, then of a sudden chastize him for no reason, often with great brutality. Frequently his morbid desires are kindled by flogging little girls and boys with rods, and then he may proceed to criminal attempts, such as seizing his victims' genitals with his hands, or other acts of violence.

In the next stage of the disease there appears a profound perturbation manifested by delirious incoherence, erroneous ideas of imminent persecution, alternating with excitation and megalomania. The patients frequently have attacks of dizziness, fainting fits, and sometimes cramps. Paralysis is not long in following, with mental torpor, impotence and apathy. The patient will permit himself to die of hunger if those about him do not take adequate care. Or else, there may set in senile pneumonia, a disease of the bladder, etc., so that the sick man is definitely confined to bed.

The disease generally takes on the chronic form and its evolution lasts several years. In exceptional instances it presents more hasty progress and may terminate in a year or a few months. The better the patient's general health, the slower will be the progress of the disorder and the longer the initial symptoms will remain limited to isolated psychic signs like contemptible avarice, extreme distrust, or baseless terror of being robbed.

When the initial symptoms are of sexual character, the patients may come to be a source of considerable danger to public morality. They seem to enjoy good physical health, are richly endowed from the point of view of mentality, have experience, knowledge, resources, and yet they satisfy their morbid instincts using the utmost caution and patience, and proceeding methodically in their work of demoralizing youth and childhood.

The foregoing does not warrant our subscribing to the metaphysical reflections of the ingenious philosopher who saw in pederasty, especially in its senile form, a new proof of nature's power of adaptation. Schopenhauer[1], we know, was struck before other observers with the frequency of sexual perversion in old men. According to him, this wide-spread prevalence at all and amongst all peoples, as well as the impossibility of extirpating it, prove that it is an innate characteristic of human nature, and he argues that only this hypothesis can explain the constant, ineluctable presence of the phenomenon observed.

He sets forth that this phenomenon is really a law by which nature strives to prevent old men from contrib-

---

1. Schopenhauer, *Die Welt als Wille und Vorstellung*, Leipzig, 1859, vol. II, §641.

uting to the propagation of the species. As Aristotle has already affirmed, old men after the age of 54 invariably engender weak, rickety children, and are thus a cause of racial deterioration.

Nature's principal goal is the propagation of the species. The individual is for her but a means to this end. And nature reveals her laws on this subject by inculcating a taste for pederasty in those whose power to procreate vigorous, healthy children has begun to decline. According to Schopenhauer the evil caused by pederasty is insignificant when compared with the evil it helps to prevent. But well-established facts contradict the paradoxical assertion of the celebrated philosopher. Pederasty, and especially senile pederasty, cause the greatest harm to society, particularly to youth and childhood.

Sometimes a patient of this sort is for years the center of a whole circle of pederasts, the leader of a whole company of psychopaths and dissolute men. He spreads the wildest license, celebrates pederastic orgies, arranges appointments for mutual flagellation, sodomy, etc. And this may go on until the progressively growing disease carries him off to the grave, or irrational acts perpetrated in broad daylight proclaim his madness.

One very clear instance of senile pederasty, with slow, continued, progressive development of senile dementia, is a case cited in Russian jurisprudence, the case of Mr. J... A man of 65 years, who occupied a very high position and had wide education, he would advise young men through the medium of the newspapers that he had clerical work for them to do. When they presented themselves, he would go in for the most cynical talk, would recommend the most indecent acts to them, finally initiating them to pederasty.

A most horrible type of senile sexual perversion associated with the vilest cruelty is that of the celebrated Marshal Gilles de Rais. Gilles de Laval, lord of Rais and a Marshal of France, was condemned at Nantes in 1440, during the reign of Charles VII, to be burned alive for outraging and murdering more than eight hundred children in the space of eight years. The sentence was executed.

He perpetrated the most unheard of cruelties upon young children of both sexes at his castle in Brittany, where he led a solitary life far from the Court. Once he was in prison, he used every means in his power to defend himself, agreeing in advance with his accomplices as to what they were to tell the judges and what they were to avoid saying. Finally, in the face of damning evidence and confronted with the admissions of his henchmen, Henriet and Pontou, he acknowledged his crime and made a confession whose details would make you turn pale. He declared that the reading of Seutonius and the description of the orgies of Tiberius, Caracalla and other Roman emperors had given him the first idea of trying to do likewise. From then on he began to entice little children to his castle with the aid of Henriet and Pontou. There he would outrage them, submit them to all sorts of tortures, and finally kill them. The dead bodies were burned, only a few pretty heads being preserved as souvenirs.

"In committing these acts," says the Marshal, "I felt an inexplicable ecstasy, evidently inspired by the Devil, and that is why I beg that I may be granted the possibility of doing penance in some cloister for my crimes."

He wrote to Charles VII to implore his clemency and acknowledged of his own accord that he had left the Court because he felt that there was being born within him an irresistible desire to violate children, and in particular the young heir to the crown.

CHAPTER TWELVE

Pederasts and Catamites
-- Russian Cases

Sexual perversion may at times be observed in progressive paralysis of the insane, and in that case constitutes an early sign of serious cerebral disorder. The public knows this affection by the general name of "softening of the brain". The gradually increasing frequency of progressive paralysis, evidently linked up with present-day social conditions, places this disease in the front rank of organic brain disorders complicated with mental aberrations, and reveals the immediate necessity for taking serious account of the symptomatology of this morbid development. The symptoms are far from being identical in all cases, whether considered anatomically or clinically.

Without going further into the description of the varieties of this clinical entity, known everywhere by the generic name of "paralytic idiocy", I must call attention to the fact that the disease may, in its premonitory period, drag on for a number of years before psy-cho-motor disturbances appear. This is in contradic-tion to the generally accepted notion that the total dur-ation of the disease does not exceed two or three years at most. In the prodromal period, during which modi-fications consist principally in disturbances of the va-so-motor system, there is a gradual, imperceptible change in the patient's character, habits and activity. Meanwhile everyone around him considers him quite sound.

At the outset of the preliminary stage it is not rare to find an increase of self-esteem, an energy much mag-nified in certain respects, combined with perversion of the sex instinct[1]. The model father of a family, sexu-ally temperate until that time, begins to frequent pros-titutes, and makes an ingenuous admission to his doc-tor that one woman is no longer enough for him. It is for this same reason that the patient has recourse to pederasty. As he himself says, the ordinary act of cop-ulation does not satisfy him, so he goes in for sodomy, then pederasty. He feels no remorse, has no percep-tion of the enormity of his doings and therefore does not repent them. Generally he goes to see a physician about some venereal disease he has contracted, and then recounts his sexual debauches and aberrations without the least hesitancy. The coolness with which he admits the vicious gratification of his passions, the in-

1. Tarnowsky, *Geschlechtsinn.*

112

genuousness of the story itself, a certain absence of shame, the indifference and scorn for the forms universally adopted for describing such subjects, all these things must naturally seem strange to the attentive observer.

More thorough examination usually reveals the appearance of other signs which, though not clearly marked, are none the less indicative of the initial stage of progressive paralysis. We can notice in the patient a certain degree of distraction, a tendency to forget things. He is insensitive to fatigue. According to his own assertion, he is always fresh, alert, cheerful. Yet in reality he is incapable of writing a couple of business letters one after the other, makes mistakes in the simplest accounts, and easily forgets proper names. He finds difficulty in fixing his mind upon a single subject. The general intelligence and memory in particular seem to be diminished. At times the patient has a tendency to congestion, with painful feeling of oppression, occasionally accompanied by fits of nausea and dizziness. These phenomena are due to growing paresis of the vaso-motor nerves. The patient often explains them by an insufficiently satisfied genital need, and gives himself up as never before to all sorts of license, among others sodomy and pederasty.

The lack of such precautions as habitual pederasts take, a certain effrontery the afflicted subjects use in proposing sex relations of the most unnatural character to prostitutes or venal catamites, then the want of perseverance in these intentions and the lack of the drive we notice in periodic attacks of perversion, all these signs distinguish paralytic pederasty from the other varieties of the same aberration. The subject will importune a woman or young boy with his unclean propositions, but if these are rejected, he will not persist in his supplications with the boldness and irrationality of an impulsive psychopath. The more the disease drags on, the more thoughtless and frantic the patient becomes.

At times he will apply to persons least likely to listen to him and will permit himself the most indecent talk and gestures. He becomes extremely cynical, yet knows perfectly well how to restrain himself when the slightest observation is made to him. Under such conditions he often figures as the hero of various affairs or causes legal proceedings to be taken against him for offending public morality.

The disease may sometimes remain for months and years in this precursory stage with alternate increase and let up, until it attains its full development and reveals itself by the unquestionable psychic and motor disorders which characterize paralysis of the insane. Megalomania, irritability or maniacal excitation, difficulty of speech, trembling of the tongue, unsureness in walking and other symptoms appear and denote a highly accentuated cerebral affection. Perturbations of the sex instinct pass into the background and the patient is given over to the care of alienists. It is evidently of primary importance to know how to ward off the disease from its very beginning, when it is not distinctly marked.

In an interesting study on the early functional disorders in progressive paralysis, Dr. Negris[1] reports the following observation. A gentleman of 52, occupied with intellectual work and leading a perfectly moral life, was arrested on the charge of attempting criminal acts upon two little girls. Subsequent examination demonstrated that evident symptoms of progressive paralysis might be detected in him, which had received no attention previously.

I recall the case of a young scholar who devoted himself to intense work and in all things observed the austerity of an ascetic. In him, the preliminary stage of the disease lasted at least two years during which it was revealed first by exaltation, then by perversion of the sex instinct. As he gradually lost his force of will and his understanding grew less and less, he continued to practice pederasty with venal catamites. He got a chancre of the penis and infected several of these catamites, but this left him completely unmoved.

As the feelings of reserve and pity become blunted, apathy progressively increases and decency grows less. These are characteristic traits of the preliminary period. A man of generous, charitable nature who took to heart his fellowman's misfortune and who preached

---

1. Negris, *De la dynamie ou exaltation fonctionnelle au début de la paralysie générale*, 1878.

the gospel of self-denial and hard work, won the love of a girl by his beneficent doings and inherent quality of character. The girl became passionately enamored of him, they soon grew more intimate and concluded by becoming engaged. Things remained this way for over a year without in any way going beyond the bounds of propriety. Then suddenly their relationship was broken off. The unhappy, forsaken girl suffered cruelly without stirring her fiancé's pity, and finally she resorted to suicide by poison. The complete indifference of the man when confronted with the tragic end of the girl who should have been so dear to him was the first apparent symptom of an incipient morbid development. A year later, exacerbation of the procreative sense became manifest, partly in the form of sodomy, and at the end of three years the unfortunate man terminated his life in an insane asylum with all the signs of regular general paralysis.

Just to complete the description, I shall add a few words here on the subject of the morbid symptoms known under the name of *priapism*. According to certain observers these should be ranged amongst the causes producing exaggeration or perversion of the sex act. Highly increased erethism, morbid sex desire with continual erection and ejaculation, lessened consciousness and a propensity to impulsive acts, these constitute the symptomatic picture of maniacal states of the various forms and intensities such as we have described above. Here is the picture of priapism: continual involuntary erection accompanied by attenuated sexual desire, absence of voluptuous sensations, rare and widely separated emissions of sperm.

Priapism may be produced in particularly acute form by intoxication with cantharides, as we have already noted. Another identical state shows up in relatively fugitive fashion during certain affections of the urogenital system, like urethritis, inflammation of the corpus cavernosum, corpus spongiosum, etc. Lastly, it may be one of the very painful symptoms of myelitis and irritation of the genito-spinal center.

In 1882 I had occasion, in the course of my clinical work at the Academy of Saint Petersburg, to observe in a soldier a case of priapism due to the latter cause. The disorder lasted two years and prevented the patient from performing active service. The patient first resorted to coitus in order to free himself from this painful state, but the chronic complete erection was not reduced after several copulations. Later on coitus and ejaculation especially were accompanied by violent pains. Sex desires and erotic ideas had entirely disappeared, and the mere thought of copulation caused the sufferer a disagreeable sensation. To a less accentuated degree I have been able to observe priapism of central origin in certain incipient cases of tabes dorsalis (locomotor ataxia).

Priapism is generally manifested with reduced sexual appetite, long-lasting erections, and ejaculation slow in arriving even during coitus, whence the extraordinary prolongation of the act. Even after it is consummated and complete sexual apathy has set in, the erection persists for a certain time. The loss of voluptuous sensation characteristic of priapism makes it impossible to recognize in this state the symptom of deviation or perversion of the sex instinct.

But there are exceptions. Priapism, as a symptom of incipient tabes, may seize upon a man who has led a life of sexual license. We must in fact remember that men who go in for venereal excesses make up an important contingent of tabes victims. The patients then attribute the diminution in pleasurable sensations and delay in ejaculation to lack of external stimulation, the jading of the senses to accustomed charms. They may resort to various new devices till then unknown to them, in order to obtain better erection and satisfaction of their desires.

The most extravagant orgies, Athenian nights, pederasty, sodomy, silver needles stuck into the erect penis or scrotal sac when erections last too long; all this ends by destroying the sexual vigor of these patients. During this time the progress of the disease makes them fall into total impotence, associated with motor disturbances of the lower limbs and other symptoms of rapidly evolving *tabes dorsalis*.

CHAPTER THIRTEEN

Etiology of Sex Perversions --Societies of Pederasts

In order to describe the principal types of aberration of the sexual sense we have divided perversions into several groups, in accordance with their clinical manifestations and what we know of their etiology. It would however be an error to think that in reality we always encounter types as well defined as the ones we have established. Between the sharply characterized extreme forms there are many different transitional varieties and combinations. A definite type may lose its characteristic traits under the influence of different conditions of life, or it may be so modified and combined with other morbid phenomena as to present itself in highly complex form.

The pederast invariably seeks the company of his own kind, for it is only with them that he may with impunity gratify his abnormal leanings, and meet with sympathy for his morbid condition as well as encouragement for his vice. Moreover, it is easier for the active pederast than for the normal individual to recognize the passive pederast by his walk, carriage, gestures, speech, looks, etc. For his own part, the catamite readily recognizes whom he has to do with by the sound of the voice. That is why pederasts so easily get into touch with one another and to a certain extent constitute societies where all the previously described types of sexual aberration are found united.

Such a community excites morbid impulses, leads them to a very high pitch of intensity and encourages the wildest license. Vicious habits join with morbid predispositions, and the imagination becomes whetted for the discovery of the most stupefying conceptions. The latter would appear to the sound mind as unsuspectable and terrifying in their indecency. The characteristic traits of morbid types mingle there and their peculiarities match one another. The catamite learns to become active pederast on occasion, and the pedicator at times plays the passive part.

Pederasts who prostitute themselves for money often undertake to play this dual role, but congenital pederasts accept this arrangement too. Yet in the latter there is always a preference for one single form of pederasty. Senile pederasts are the ones who show themselves to be the most inventive in imagining new variants of the vice, by combining it with flagellation, mutual masturbation, and so on. This is especially true where senile dementia has developed in a soil of sexual perversion.

In all congenital pederasts sexual excitation is pathologically magnified by reason of irritable debility of the nervous system. As a result, erection quickly terminates in ejaculation, and the sex act is thus promptly concluded. The desire to make the erethism last as long as possible drives such patients to avoid the act itself, and to seek gratification of their senses in various touches and caresses. They go in particularly for all sorts of onanistic practices with the object of their passion. In time this habit becomes more and more inveterate. The erethism reaches its peak and ends in an orgasm before the actual performance of the pederastic act. The latter may even come to be superfluous, and often is made impossible because of incomplete erection or disease of the rectal canal.

In this way the active or passive pederast may gradually be transformed into a *fellator*, that is to say, in order to satisfy his sex desires he practices coitus *ab ore* (oral coitus) instead of rectal coitus. Tardieu[1] describes them in this way: "Qui labia et oscula fellatricuibus blanditiis praebant". This phase of homosexuality may be manifested in relatively young subjects, and is propagated especially by example and common usage in clubs of pederasts. These clubs constitute powerful sources for the diffusion of moral depravity.

---

1. Tardieu, *loc. cit.*, p.206.

Pederasts and Mannish Women

Both active and passive pederasts show extreme variation in the intensity of the impulsion and attraction they feel towards pederasty. Some are entirely incapable of having normal relations with women. Others, on the contrary, are capable under fixed conditions, as for example when the woman has a mannish appearance. In the latter case the person's sex sometimes loses its importance, by reason of the frequent alternations between boys and young women. Inclination towards a certain person and sexual excitation are then induced by physiognomic traits, and the sex is quite immaterial. A turned up nose, a rounded chin with a dimple, sensual lips, big eyes, a very ruddy complexion, any one of these may make the person desirable. When it comes to a woman, they prefer one with comparatively undeveloped breasts and pelvis; the waist must not be too narrow, and to a certain extent must recall that of a boy. If it is a question of a man, he must be neither too tall nor have too highly developed muscles. He must offer the general effect of a woman's appearance. In fact, there come to be certain necessary traits: the power of imagination creates a particular type of beauty in which the sex has very little importance. The face is then the main thing, and some chosen body-form becomes secondary.

When such individuals have to do with youngsters, they do not always practice sodomy upon them. Some even avoid this, since they consider that it deprives them of the sight of their favorite's face. Therefore they obtain ejaculation by rubbing the penis between the thighs of the catamite who lies supine, after the manner of women. In France a special name was coined to designate this act, which was known to the Romans, too.

These inverts tend to avoid women, but only because their morbidly overwrought erethism so diminishes the duration of the act that they are incapable of satisfying a healthy woman. Besides, in catamites, particularly congenital ones, the orgasm is brought on not only by friction, but by mere contact with the beloved person, and naturally even more so by the procedure described above. Despite these things, such individuals sometimes transmit some degree of their sexual perversion. They continue to feel love for boys and may carry on amorous intrigues simultaneously with young men and young women.

I knew one pederast who had relations exclusively with young boys. At a relatively advanced age he fell passionately in love with a young woman by whom he had several children. Yet he could perform the procreative act only with this woman, because her features reminded him of those of a young man he had formerly loved. Another invert, on the very day of his marriage to a beautiful young girl, became so ardently enamored of a young boy he noticed that he abandoned the projected marriage, and from that moment on set aside all relations with women and took to gratifying his senses with the form of coitus described just before.

It is to be noted that certain inverts make exclusive use

of this latter procedure to satisfy their senses, or as a variation on sodomy. But most individuals of this category consider it as only a preparatory step towards anal coition, particularly when they meet a young man susceptible to becoming a catamite. In such cases the seducer always employs the utmost caution, above all when he is an acquired pederast in whom the impulsive character of the act is wanting, and whose willpower is not morbidly diminished. The same applies to the early stages of senile pederasty where the understanding and self-control are still intact. It is only in the most pronounced degrees of degeneration, in morbid impulsion, maniacal excitation or in the late forms of senile dementia that there is brutality in the performance of the act of pederasty, or the use of violence without previous preparatory measures.

We must likewise note that fear of syphilitic infection sometimes brings about the transformation of a slight pederastic tendency into absolute pederasty. Pederasts are generally inclined to believe that syphilitic infection can not accompany sodomy, and that serves to explain their attachment to this form of sexual gratification. It is needless to say that such a supposition is fundamentally wrong. The same types of syphilis may be acquired through pederasty as through regular intercourse with women. Nevertheless, it often happens that subjects called accidental pederasts, after having contracted a chancre or urethritis from a woman, will renounce all relations with women through fear of new infection. They may thus become incorrigible pederasts, especially when they can practice their vice with ease.

CHAPTER FOURTEEN

Pederasty Among Roman Emperors

Roman Magnification of Sexuality

THE history of the Roman emperors furnishes us with numerous examples of the most absolute, most unbridled sex perversion, where acquired immorality and boundless license developed on an hereditary soil. We find there the most complex forms of sexual aberration whose rise was protected by highly favorable conditions. Congenital predisposition, vicious education, the absence of all morality in the environment, everything, in short, favored the development of the most aggravated and most complicated varieties of sexual aberration. But still, a careful examination of what their illustrious contemporaries have handed down on this score permits us to recognize in their general traits the principal types of sexual perversion that we have described. From the time of Julius Caesar until the time of Diocletian, we have before us a series of pathologic subjects who are extremely interesting and instructive from the sexual point of view.

Rampant Vices of the Caesars

Julius Caesar was the nephew of the famous Marius, conqueror of the Cimbrians and Teutons, an inveterate drunkard who died of alcoholism. Caesar himself was afflicted with epilepsy and had exaggerated sex instincts, as is shown by the prodigious number of concubines he kept. It is well-known that he wanted to promulgate a law by which all the women of Rome would be freely at his disposal, so as to multiply the number of scions of his great and glorious line. Later on when his sexual potency declined, he became a passive pederast, which made Curio call him: *Omnium virorum mulierem et omnium mulierum virum.*

Tiberius is a clearly defined type of the licentious man whose life ends in senile dementia. While on the island of Capri, Tiberius' cruelty was gradually replaced by refinements of depravity, but towards the close of the emperor's long life, the island's exports of corpses of little boys and girls tortured to death by the diseased old man far exceeded the exports of flowers and fragrant spices.

Vitellius, heir to the throne, was brought up on Capri by Tiberius. From his childhood on he went through a real course of induction into vice in the company of several other young boys who were taught to fill the functions of catamites, beginning with the role of "pisciculi", whom Tiberius liked so much. (See C. Suetonius Tranquillus, *De vita Caesarum,* Tiberius XLIV) Vitellius became an habitual pederast, and once he had ascended the throne, he lived openly with the freed slave, Asiaticus. He concluded his life in complete idiocy.

The innate form of passive pederasty is very plainly visible in Heliogabalus. Called to the throne of the empire, he made solemn entry to Rome in a long silk robe, half-feminine in style, his face covered with rouge and his eyebrows painted. He was fond of putting on women's apparel, having himself called "Empress", and entrusted the management of his affairs to his favorites, recruited from amongst the gladiators, athletes and actors. He himself used to dress his lovers, would have some of them castrated after the Oriental fashion, and would practice inversion as a fellator.

Passive pederasty also had its representative in the emperor Hadrian, whose amorous intrigue with the handsome Antinous is well known. The psychopathic state of this emperor is fully revealed in the following character description given by one of his contemporaries: "Good alternates with evil in him. At times he is gentle, then cruel without reason. He is either benevolent or irritable and vindictive. The dissoluteness of his morals gives way to remorse. Humility and manifestations of morbid self-love, justness and brutality succeed one another." Such contradictions of character, noted so clearly that they strike present-day historians, are entirely in accord with the pathologic effects of psychic degeneration.

Hadrian was a cousin of Trajan, who was well known

as a drunkard and active pederast. Such was the latter's reputation that upon his accession to the throne, Jupiter was warned not to let Ganymedes out of his sight.

Nero, who was already a very pronounced type of neuropath by heredity from his mother, Agrippina, combined in himself congenitally exaggerated sexual impulsiveness and vicious development, together with a certain amount of culture. The latter condition widened the range of manifestations of his pathological activity. After having violated a vestal virgin, he had the young Sporus castrated, attired in women's clothes and then solemnly married him. He used to practice inconceivable cruelties upon the women with whom he had relations, and at the same time yielded as passive pederast to his freed slave Doryphorus. Towards the end of his reign he wedded a young eunuch. Previously he had gotten himself married as wife to an actor.

We shall not go into greater detail. They can be found clearly and precisely reported by Suetonius in his "History of the Twelve Caesars", by Petronius (master of fashions, contemporary of Nero and organizer of his orgies), Martial, Juvenal and other authors. We merely wanted to demonstrate how the principal traits of certain types of sexual perversion, even in such remote times, as well as the terrible moral depravity which excited them, have remained much the same to our own day. In spite of the unlimited freedom of desire, the force and omnipotence of vice push-

ed to the utmost bounds of demoralization, despite
license ultra-refined by science and the ingenuity of
servile talents, this cloaca of all imaginable sensual
debauchery shows pathologic types which retain their
precise character and a remarkable similarity in their
manifestations. The all-powerful Roman emperor displays the same aberrations in his lusts as we may now-
adays observe in an individual for whom Romans and
sexual perversion are dead letters. A common Russian
soldier, A. M. . ., discharged from service, devoid of
education and culture, certainly incapable of understanding the meaning of virtue and vice, was arraigned
before the criminal court in Saint Petersburg under
indictment for acts entirely similar to those indulged
in by Tiberius.

In the sphere of demoralization and license, neither
the creative genius nor the philosophical intellect has
given birth to anything really new, special or original
which stands out from surrounding things. Pathologic
manifestations alone bear the stamp of real strangeness, of comparative originality. It is only they that
present certain special traits, according to whether the
sex instinct is overwrought or on the wane. Moral depravation in healthy subjects, fully cognizant of their
vice, engenders but a very small number of new forms
from the sexual standpoint, and borrows its expres-
sions principally from morbid subjects.

The subtle refinements of demoralization in the Romans at the time of the decadence may be attributed

mainly to imitation of certain psychopaths who served as models. "Lunatics at large", one historian calls them, for they were subject to no restraint, their sense of decency was obnubilated, their sexuality magnified. They openly indulged in the most licentious acts without being at all aware of their demoralization. And the example of the upper classes incited the others, making it possible for everyone to satisfy abnormal appetites.

CHAPTER FIFTEEN

Antiquity of Pederasty-- Pederastic Blackmail --Russian Officials

IF we leave antiquity to consider present times, we must notice that a certain leniency towards sexual abnormality favors propagation of the vice. We cannot, however, use this to explain the periodic outbreaks of sex perversion in various places. The primary conditions for the existence of pederasty (whether the result of psychic degeneration in the form of congenital sexual perversion, or as symptom of senile dementia, progressive paralysis, epileptic psychoses, etc.) may very well have been present at all times and among all peoples. In India, China and Japan pederasty was well known and described several centuries before this form of perversion had invaded Persia and Greece. The opinion that pederasty as an epidemic came out of the Orient to Greece, from there to Rome, and thence spread all over Europe, is not strictly accurate. Pederasty has been observed as a morbid manifestation at all times and in all countries, and where the conditions of social life have favored development of general psychic degeneration, there has been more propagation of sexual anomalies, and pederasty among them. Then again, it is easy to understand that during the period when a nation's intellectual activity is at its height and reaches out into all branches of art, science and industry, when as a result of keener competition the struggle for life becomes more intense and everything conspires to produce greater nervous tension, during such a time more favorable conditions are set up for the development of an hereditary neuropathic constitution with multiple forms of sexual perversion. That is why we may often observe an increase of sexual aberration parallel with a rapid advance in civilization. The depravation which formerly played a separate part in sexual perversion is now linked up with the rapid development of intellectual culture, and brings on an augmentation of mental and nervous diseases in direct ratio to the speed of intellectual progress. But I repeat that pederasty, which is spontaneously manifested in isolated cases, attains the proportions of a social plague when favored by certain circumstances. This is particularly true where the vicious taste finds conditions propitious for its satisfaction. Generally these same conditions will favor the acquired form of the vice.

In Russia, notably in Saint Petersburg, there are many bathing establishments containing numerous private rooms. These have a regular staff of attendants, among whom there are many mercenary pederasts forming private associations, so to speak. In France, England and Italy the invert is always in dread of finding the catamite to be a denouncer or master-extortioner. Procurers who go in for such business are not aways able to guarantee the discretion of the subjects they supply. That is why pederasty in London, Paris, and Rome demands absolute secrecy, requires considerable expense and is always accompanied by fear of blackmail. For a certain time in Paris there was also organized surveillance of male prostitution, and an "under-squad of pederasts" was attached to the medical staff of the police.

A catamite in Saint Petersburg receives about the same fee as a prostitute. Blackmail on the part of bath-house boys is practically unknown, because they operate by associations and share the profits. Aside from bath-house attendants the ranks of catamites are recruited from amongst young coachmen, janitors, apprentices in the various trades who have not been working for a long time, etc. According to what all pederasts have told me, uneducated common people in Saint Petersburg appear to be extremely indulgent to indecent solicitations. These are "gentlemen's pleasures", they say. These simple creatures do not consider such propositions as at all insulting, and whether they accept or decline them, they would never denounce them of their own initiative, or complain about them to the authorities.

I knew an active pederast who was for years in the habit of seducing young door-keepers. His advances were of course often repulsed, sometimes even roughly, but not one of these young men ever struck fear into him by threatening to lodge a complaint. Another invert was accustomed to making similar propositions, with the same results, while inspecting vacant apartments. He would always choose young assistant-porters for this purpose. A third pederast used to operate more particularly upon young coachmen. He would chat with them during the trip, would promote their acquaintance, would visit their lodgings, and never met with any mishap. They would accept or turn down his propositions, but always good-naturedly.

Four years ago a former soldier, Alexis M . ., aged 55, was prosecuted before the district court in Saint Petersburg. He was accused of having excited three of his young apprentices to perform anal and oral coition. One of the victims, W. Tsch . ., in whom the judicial investigation disclosed undeniable signs of passive pederasty and who frankly admitted the whole affair, testified as follows: "A short time ago I came from a village to Saint Petersburg. I did not know what the general practice of this place might be, so I didn't complain. In fact I supposed that all masters acted the same way here."

The common people show equal indulgence to the

propositions of congenital or senile pederasts. Generally the number of active pederasts far exceed that of passive ones. I am of the opinion that the previously mentioned facility for satisfying the vice may in part explain the rapid increase in the number of pederasts in Russia, especially in those individuals where the bent is acquired. This fact has not escaped the attention of other observers.[1]

It is nonetheless a fact that many subjects who are thus induced give up their vicious practices at the first opportunity and never return to them. But there are others (luckily but a small minority) who develop into the disgusting, utterly demoralized type of mercenary catamite we have already mentioned. In this connection, the higher the degree of education, the greater is the moral failure.

Young men who have fallen into the hands of pederasts upon leaving school and become catamites, quickly grow accustomed to squandering their easily gotten gains. As they progress along the road of depravation and crime, they may abandon pederasty as an insufficiently remunerative profession. Others who are cleverer may combine pederasty with blackmail.[2] In all large cities like London, Paris, Berlin, Vienna there have been important trials for pederasty and black-

---

1. See Krauss, *loc. cit.*, p. 176.
2. Mémoires of Canler (ex-chief of the secret service), chap. XXXIII, *Les Antiphysiques et les chanteurs*, p.264, Brussels, 1862.

mail. "S'occuper de politique" is a technical term in the argot of Parisian pederasts meaning to go in for blackmailing. Youngsters of 10 and 12 are made to go astray by persuasion and threats, and led into masturbation and sodomy. Then they are inducted into the profession of catamite-informer. They are known as "les petits jésus". Some dismissed policeman or discharged detective, who has retained a few connections with headquarters, is usually at the head of such an affair. They are creatures fallen to the lowest depths of infamy and vice. The mercenary catamite merely plays the part of a decoy.

It is in Russia that this sort of blackmail is least common. Among the examples set forth by Dr. Mierzejewski the case of Mr. M .. presents a certain interest. In fact it offers an analogy to other legal matters of the same category subsequently tried in foreign countries, although here the immediate connection of the principal party with the police chiefs remains unexplained. The case of Mr. M .. depicts a class of Russian society which is represented by mercenary catamites, aside from the bath-house boys. I shall conclude the description of the principal varieties of sexual perversion by a rapid review of this affair in which we may see the basest, most infamous expression of mercenary pederasty and extortion by blackmail.

In 1870 an accusation of pederasty was brought against a person occupying a high place in the administrative circles of Saint Petersburg. The man was im-

mediately dismissed from his governmental functions
and exiled, without the case having been heard or
tried before a court of law. The denouncer was a mercenary pederast, the son of a coachman. He was of
rather weak mind, a shameless boy without education
or calling.

Much was said about the affair. The victim was married, had children, and was esteemed as a model father of a family. He was a man of brilliant, cultivated
intellect, had a splendid career ahead of him, and lost
it all through the denunciation of an obscure vagrant.
This occurrence could not fail to have a particular influence upon mercenary pederasts. They realized that
all that was needed, when the opportunity came up,
was to terrify some official personage by threatening to
make accusations of pederasty. Dread of losing his
situation would then make the victim come to terms
and pay to avoid being denounced. The most infamous
extortion of hush-money became established.

The principal figure in the case was a youth of 17
who had just left high school and lived with his mother, a poor woman who barely managed to exist upon a
monthly allowance of 25 roubles granted by one of
her relatives. In the meantime M. began to show off at
hotels and restaurants where he was a steady visitor,
and where they knew him by the name of Mitroschka.
He would dress in a blouse of crimson silk with a blue
sash, cloaked by an overcoat. He squandered money on

droshkys, billiards, in cafés. He was seen with as much as three hundred roubles in his hands.

His accomplices were youths without occupation or resources. Some were arraigned with him, the others were dismissed by the court for lack of evidence. One of them was P., 17 years of age, son of a pensioned sergeant who conducted a small commission-business. P. lived with his father. Another, aged 19, had first been a singer, then a household servant, but he had lost his job. A third, 25 years old, had been a bell-hop. The fourth was an unemployed clerk; the fifth, 21 years old, was a tailor without work, and so on.

All of them used to meet daily in a well-known restaurant where they and their nicknames were familiar to the waiters. There they would strike up an acquaintance with newly arrived travelers and appointments would be made. Generally M. would hire a room at a bathing establishment together with the prospective victim. Then after a short while one of the accomplices would break in and start making a scene, threatening to denounce the victim to the secret police with accusations of pederasty. In the end the accomplice would let himself be appeased by a certain payment of hush-money, and would agree not to carry the thing any further. The racketeers would then divide up the money. The victim naturally kept quiet for fear of arousing the slightest suspicion of his repugnant vice.

Everything came to light through a case where the confederates combined theft with blackmail. Under cir-

cumstances like those described above, M. stole a
watch and chain, together with a pocketbook containing money and visiting cards from Mr. J., an official
who had just arrived in Saint Petersburg. Two days
later M. dined with his accomplices at one of the best
restaurants, leaving one of Mr. J.'s personal cards as
guaranty of payment for the bill. At the same time he
signed J.'s name to the note required by the restaurant
owner. When they called at Mr. J.'s to collect on the
note, he went to the police commissioner and complained of having been victim of a robbery, expressing
his fear that the thieves might continue the misuse of
his name.

A legal investigation was instituted and M. was im-
prisoned. He started out by declaring that Mr. J. had
made attempts to lead him into sodomy, and cited the
names of some other persons who according to him
likewise went in for pederasty. A few days later the
same M. also made accusations to the secret police a-
gainst another administrative officer, Mr. B., recently
arrived, as having induced him to practice sodomy.
Shortly afterwards, another complaint was lodged with
the commissioner of police by a member of the government, Mr.E. He stated that two young men had presented themselves at his home saying they were secret-
service agents, and had extorted money from him by
threatening to bring accusations of pederasty, if he did
not give in to their demands. Mr. E. gave them some
money, but foreseeing that this hold-up would be re-

peated, he notified the police. It was established that M. was one of the young men who had extorted the money from Mr. E.

But the audacity of these master-blackmailers was applied with even greater cost to another government official, B. They went to his office and demanded payment of a sum of money, for want of which they threatened to denounce him as a pederast. Several times B. was weak enough to yield to their threats and gave them a lump sum of twenty-five roubles. After that they began to show up incessantly in the ante-room of his office, and their demands began to exceed all bounds. Orders were given to refuse them admittance to the office, but then they went to his private residence and asked for his brother, to whom they announced that unless they received immediate payment of fifty roubles they would lodge a complaint against Mr. B. as a pederast.

In the end M. was recognized as guilty of stealing somewhat less than three hundred roubles, and of extorting money by means of threats and false accusations. He was sentenced to six months in prison.[1]

---

1. Mierzejewski, *Legal Gynecology* (in Russian), cases 36 and 37, p.252.

CHAPTER SIXTEEN

Sexual Problems of Law Courts

UNTIL lately, legal medicine has grouped all forms of pederasty under the common heading of sodomy, without even attaching any particular importance to the subdivision of the latter into the active and passive forms, taking it for granted that the two always went hand in hand. Most physicians attributed pederasty to such causes as exaggerated sexual appetite, demoralization, satiation of erotic desires. It is quite difficult for the medico-legal expert to free himself from this way of thinking, especially when we consider that trials for pederasty most of the time present a mass of extremely immoral acts. And this stands out clearly in the works of Casper and of Tardieu, whose studies on the subject have until now been considered as classics. Casper, for example, relates the following episode. A janitor named F. perpetrated onanistic acts upon five children in the most abominable manner, but without practicing masturbation upon himself. The prisoner's skull was remarkable for its resemblance to a monkey's. The forehead was absolutely flat, the malar bones and upper maxillary forming a pronounced protrusion.

Two months later a schoolmaster named F. was accused of identical acts committed upon two little boys and three little girls. He, too, had an oddly shaped head. The malar bones and upper maxillary were very prominent, and the posterior part of the skull was in the form of an arch. This conformation was so striking that the prisoner was submitted to my examination in order to ascertain whether it might explain the nature of his crime. I called attention to the simian skull conformation of the recently convicted F., which so exactly resembled the one under observation, but I nevertheless refused to draw any conclusion from that. The culprit was sentenced to imprisonment for several years.[1]

Tardieu, who wrote a highly documented monograph on pederasty, nevertheless says at the close of his work: "No matter how incomprehensible and unnatural the acts may be which spring from pederasty, still they cannot escape the responsibility of conscience, the just severity of the laws, and above all, the scorn of decent persons.[2]

---

1. Casper, *Praktisches Handbuch der gerichtlichen Medizin,* Berlin, 1880, p.199.
2. Tardieu, *loc. cit.,* p.206.

Criminal Punishment of Psychopaths

When we study the matter more closely, we see that it is impossible to expect remorse of conscience on the part of a congenital catamite, who from the first a-wakening of his sex instinct has felt and known no other sex urge than that of pederasty. It should certainly appear not less unjust to apply the full severity of the law to a morbid subject in whom the initial symptoms of a long, cruel disease are manifested in the form of pederastic assaults. Similarly, if we regard such impulsive acts as resulting less from malicious intent than a sick mind, it is evident that an epileptic pederast must inspire us more with sadness and pity than with scorn, just as we feel towards subjects afflicted with dipsomania and other forms of mental aberration. If it is a question of a psychopathic child with morbid sex instincts, it is not so much punishment for the vice that is to be prescribed, as appropriate education and treatment. Individuals afflicted with incipient progressive paralysis, or senile dementia, even more imperatively require medical aid instead of castigation. In all these forms it is possible to attenuate the morbid condition or to cure it. Then again, we may make the sick man inoffensive to society by isolating him, and in that case, too, a penalty for immoral acts would not be applicable. Such subjects are of neuropathic constitution, victims of a mental and nervous disorder. They are not criminals.

Among the numerous instances of manifestly diseased individuals who have been convicted, I shall cite the following cases which came up in France some years ago. A man named R. assassinated an old woman of 53 and violated the corpse. He then threw the body into a river, but shortly afterwards fished it out of the water to repeat the act upon it. R. was convicted and executed. Dr. Evrard, who performed the autopsy on his body, discovered numerous morbid modifications in the brain and meninges, such as considerable thickening of the latter with adhesions to the frontal circumvolutions, etc. Dr. Cornil, who reports the fact, adds this judicious remark: "If the law courts consider the guillotine as a curative agent for treating insanity, then this fact ought to be generally known."

In the Menesclou case, which we have alluded to previously, a manifestly diseased subject was guillotined in consequence of the gross error of the medico-legal experts, an error demonstrated by the autopsy on the poor man's brain. It is only real vice, acquired sex perversion in a healthy man (particularly the vice represented by mercenary catamites) which deserves fitting punishment. And here we may ask whether the same sort of penalty should be applied to a simple, weak-minded farm-hand, accidentally led astray, as to the confirmed, mercenary catamite, totally depraved and demoralized. But however that may be, punishment is the logical procedure in cases of acquired pederasty.

The result of all these considerations is that the technical examination of pederasty is for the present extremely complicated. The expert has not only to decide whether or not the subject is an invert, but also to determine precisely what form of sex perversion he is confronted with. I shall devote a few words here to this subject.

CHAPTER SEVENTEEN

Physical Examinations for Pederasty

THE primary question is this: Is it possible to recognize a pederast with absolute certainty by means of external signs? We can answer in the affirmative with regard to the passive form. It is undoubtedly much easier to distinguish the catamite amidst the various kinds of sexual perverts by the deformations which may be observed in the anal orifice and adjoining regions. These deformations taken by themselves are not entirely characteristic, but when studied together with other peculiarities, they present a sharply defined picture which makes diagnosis easy after a little practice.

In books on this subject (even in a monograph as well written as Tardieu's work) the signs of sodomy are described separately, and a description of the general aspect of the changes which may be noted in the average catamite is lacking. This circumstance has led many inexperienced observers in this field of investigation to deny the existence of absolute signs. Casper and Brouardel, for example, deny the importance of the dilated, infundibuliform anus which Tardieu has so particularly stressed. We must also consider the fact that the conditions under which medico-legal experts make their examinations are fundamentally different from those under which clinicians make theirs. In the presence of the former, subjects will often endeavor to conceal the existing modifications, or to simulate the ones which are lacking. The subject neither hides nor simulates anything in the presence of the clinician. To me that explains how certain modifications which appear extremely noteworthy to the practitioner receive inadequate consideration in medico-legal diagnoses.

The latter may be partly attributed to the fact that the medico-legal expert can not bring the same skill to his examination of the anal orifice as is done by the specialist who must daily look over several dozen patients, giving special attention to the rectum, frequent site of syphilitic infections. Besides, the medico-legal expert only rarely has to examine a catamite or two, and then at long intervals, whereas the practitioner is often obliged to examine a whole series of them on the same day. I may mention that during the past winter I was appointed in conjunction with my colleague, Dr. Seweke, to examine the pupils of an educational institution where syphilitic infection had broken out. We had in a single day to examine twenty-nine passive pederasts, 9 to 15 years of age, among whom we found twenty-three showing the most irrefutable signs of sodomy. The carefully noted and oft-checked results of such examinations warrant my modifying somewhat the evident signs of sodomy as they are indicated in various works and manuals.

We will begin with the habitual practicers of passive pederasty. First of all I shall give a collective description of the deformations noted in catamites 10 to 16 years of age, then I shall go on to the description of each particular symptom. The young boy submitted to examination should be placed on his knees upon a wide cot, with his chest applied against a bolster so that the head is situated a little lower than his posterior, which should be thrust forward. The legs should be spread apart and pushed as far as possible from one another. In this position the subject to be examined, if he is ignorant of the purpose of the investigation, and has no intention of hiding or simulating anything, will distinctly reveal the signs of habitual sodomy. When the legs are sufficiently wide apart, they are made unable to come into contact with the buttocks, and the anus thus becomes exposed to view.

The anus no longer presents the appearance of two cutaneous surfaces united in the same plane by the sphincter, but rather that of an infundibuliform depression. The walls of this depression begin at the outer and lower border of the sphincter and continue funnel-

wise towards the bottom, narrowing down by degrees
to the apex. Or we may describe these walls as starting
in the upper contracted layers of the sphincter and
spreading out gradually as they descend, becoming
transformed into the epidermis which surrounds the
anus and which in the normal state forms a series of
radial folds about the circumference of the orifice.
These radial folds are obliterated in the catamite and
consequently the transition between the edge of the
sphincter and the inner face of the buttocks is lacking.

When the catamite has been placed in the designated
position and the buttocks have been somewhat spread
apart by exerting pressure with the thumbs of both
hands, the funnel-shaped anal orifice opens propor-
tionately and the rectal walls become visible. This wi-
dening of the orifice resulting from relaxation of both
the outer and the inner layers of the sphincter is to my
mind the most characteristic proof. There are some
catamites in whom we cannot always observe this, but
when it does exist, the subject is undoubtedly an individual who goes in habitually for passive pederasty.

If we proceed still further, digital exploration of the
rectum reveals considerable relaxation of the anal
sphincter. The finger introduced into the rectum is not
gripped by the sphincter, and in fact two fingers could
just as easily have been introduced. It often happens
that probing with the index causes pain as a result of
slight excoriations at the anal border, where the outer
epidermis fuses with the rectal mucous membrane.

Therefore, when the subject under examination has been placed in the position indicated, and we witness an infundibuliform anal cavity, with obliteration of the radial folds, if we find that spreading apart the buttocks readily produces gaping of the anal aperture, and that touching the rectum does not bring about contraction of the sphincter, then we have, no doubt, to do with a catamite. This is especially true when it has been demonstrated that prior to the examination the individual has never undergone any surgical operation upon the anus or rectum.

But these distinguishing marks may easily be concealed under various circumstances. We shall briefly cite a few of them. The catamite in order to dissimulate his condition, may press his buttocks tightly against each other and in this way cause contraction of the sphincter and anal levator muscles. In such cases, too, when it is necessary to make the anal orifice clearly visible, we must forcibly separate the buttocks, if it becomes apparent that the cavity formed by the drawing-in of the anus results from contraction of the anal levator. A similar aspect may also be seen in normal subjects when a vigorous muscular contraction is accompanied by forced separation of the nates. I have often led confirmed catamites to squeeze the nates one against the other and to contract the muscles of the anus by pressing the thighs together. In this condition, when the nates are forcibly spread apart, the characteristic changes in the anus due to muscular relaxation were no longer visible. Therefore, probing may give quite different results according to whether the subject examined has or has not contracted the anal muscles.

In order to avoid errors of this sort, I have taken care to study how long a 16 year old catamite could keep the sphincter and anal muscles contracted, when placed in the described position, kneeling with his legs spread apart. I have noticed that at the end of 10 minutes, against the patient's will, there supervened a temporary relaxation of the contracted muscles and the characteristic modifications became fully evident. After 15 minutes, the nates would spread apart and it was only at intervals that the anal aperture was slightly constricted and drawn in by contraction of the levator, for at the time of this drawing-in a slight separation of the nates would provoke the typical anal hiatus. Each change in position by the subject brought on a delay in this, because the fatigued muscles had time to recover some strength. That is why it seems to me easier to manage a catamite by tiring him (keeping him in the same genu-pectoral position for 10 to 15 minutes) than by continually making him change his posture during examination, as Tardieu recommends. Moreover, the aforementioned observation of voluntary contraction followed by relaxation in the catamite invalidates the opinion lately expressed by Professor Brouardel regarding the formation of the infundibuliform anus.[1]

---

1.   Brouardel, *Etude critique sur la valeur des signes attribués à la pédérastie.* Annales d'hygiène publique, 1880, p.182.

The funnel-shaped depression of the anus in catamites which Cullerier had already drawn attention to, and which Tardieu considered as the most patent proof of passive pederasty, cannot be explained exclusively by contraction of the levator ani, as Brouardel supposes. It is easy to convince oneself of this, if one considers that the characteristic infundibulum opens up in the catamite when the sphincter and levator are both relaxed. Contraction of these muscles, on the other hand, invariably attenuates this special sign consisting of a distinctly infundibuliform anal depression. When the nates are spread apart by force, this anal depression is transformed into a narrow slit, such as may be seen in any normal subject, but which Brouardel has wrongly taken to be the typical infundibuliform depression.

The funnel-shaped anus is not at all brought on by contraction of the levator muscle, but exclusively by modification of the sphincter. When a voluminous penis penetrates the aperture of the rectum, the lower parts of the sphincter being weaker give way more easily under the pressure, while the stronger, upper portions contract energetically and to a certain extent oppose penetration into the rectum itself. Consequently, once the penis is introduced, it pushes the upper muscular layers farther into the rectum. It may dilate the lower sphincteral portions by about 4 centimetres in width but it encounters greater resistance on reaching the upper muscular layers. When the act has been repeated several times, the lower part of the muscle is dilated and constitutes the base of the infundibulum delimited by the inner rim of the nates. During this time the upper layers of the sphincter muscle are thrust upwards and backwards in the form of a thin ring which locks the entrance to the rectum and constitutes the apex of the funnel.

As Martineau[1] has justly observed, the process by which the infundibuliform anus is developed is precisely similar to the one whereby an identical depression is produced in the external genitalia of little girls subjected to repeated criminal assaults, or in adult women who have intercourse with a man of extraordinarily large parts. The vulvar infundibulum is formed at the expense of the constrictor muscle of the vagina, just as the anal infundibulum is exclusively formed by repeated pressure exerted upon the sphincter.

The more gradually the catamite has grown accustomed to sodomy, and the more voluminous the organ introduced, the larger will be the funnel-shaped depression. Its base is continually enlarged about the anal orifice at the expense of the radial cutaneous folds, which are progressively obliterated. But I repeat that the symptom just described has its full value only when it becomes distinctly visible without forcible separation of the nates, or else when they are but slightly

---

1. Martineau, *Leçons sur les déformations vulvaires et anales,* Paris, 1884.

spread apart. If it is necessary to separate the nates by force, in order to expose the anus to view, then the funnel sign loses its significance. Should the buttocks be forced apart, in a normal individual who voluntarily contracts the anal orifice, there always comes a time when the lower portions of the sphincter are displayed and the entrance to the rectum is closed only by the upper sphincteral layers. At this moment the anal opening forms a long, deep slit which is quite similar to the infundibuliform anus.

It is just because he has confused the infundibulum, existing when the anal muscles are relaxed, with the narrow, slit-like depression produced when the nates are separated and the sphincter and levator are contracted, that Brouardel has been led to question the diagnostic value of the infundibuliform anus, and to maintain that this sign may be met with in cases where the anus is irritated by cold, painful fissures, inflamed hemorrhoidal swellings, etc. Besides, we must take into account the fact that even an accentuated infundibuliform anus loses its distinctive character and becomes transformed into a narrow, slit-like depression when the nates are forced apart and there is contraction of the anal muscles. The infundibuliform anus may also completely escape examination in very fat catamites, having highly developed buttocks close-pressed against each other. Anyway, the absence of the funnel-shaped anus is certainly not adequate proof against the existence of passive pederasty. We may also find it lacking in very lean subjects in whom the anal orifice is nearly on the same level as the scarcely developed buttocks, and whose sphincter is quite thin.

There are even confirmed catamites in whom the funnel-shaped depression is only slightly indicated and indistinctly circumscribed. Likewise, when the organ introduced is of small dimensions, the infundibulum may be missing in an adult subject, despite frequent repetition of the sodomistic act. Lastly, in senile passive pederasts the infundibuliform anus may sometimes be quite indistinct because of numerous protrusions of hemorrhoidal swellings, and prolapse of the anus may at times make it so difficult to discern that it becomes impossible to base a diagnosis upon this symptom. From what we have just said it must be obvious that the infundibuliform anus can have only a relative value for diagnosis of sodomy, and not an absolute value as Tardieu supposed.

Another classic sign of sodomy is obliteration of the radial folds about the periphery of the anus. The Latin satirists called this *"podice laevi"*. It is a symptom upon which Zacchias placed particular emphasis as far back as the seventeenth century. Even the sceptical Casper did not deny its importance, and Tardieu rated it highly. There is no doubt that any practitioner can settle the question asked by Casper about the etiology of the above symptom. Any physician will affirm that this deformation is brought about not by the fatty ointments pederasts employ, but by the repeated expansion of the anus and surrounding epidermis caused by the sodomistic act itself. Persons afflicted with chronic constipation sometimes make daily practice of intra-anal inunction with fatty substances, and may make constant use of enemas over a long stretch of years. The same applies to patients suffering from eczema in the vicinity of the anus. Yet despite this the radial per-ianal folds are not obliterated in these patients, be-cause anointment by itself and careful introduction of a canula, cannot produce stretching of the skin adjoin-ing the anus.

However, the absence of these radial folds is, in my opinion, of only slight importance, when considered by itself. I have often noticed in well-built muscular young men, possessing a fleshy gluteal region, that if the nates are kept spread apart, the perianal cutane-ous folds were absent, although these subjects had nev-er indulged in sodomy. Then again in notorious cat-amites I have sometimes verified the presence of these radial folds conjointly with a very pronounced infund-ibulum. Out of the 23 catamites whom I examined to-gether with Dr. Seweke, and who showed undeniable signs of passive pederasty, there were only 12 in whom the radial folds were completely effaced, whereas in the remaining 11 they were perfectly discernible.

A much more significant indication for the diagnosis of passive pederasty is no doubt atony of the sphinc-ter. This is perceptible upon introduction of the index finger. Where sodomy has actually been practiced and rectal intromission of the penis has been frequently repeated, the first sign that shows up is relaxation of the sphincter. But it requires a certain amount of practice to recognize this symptom, when taken by itself, and in cases which are not chronic. As I have every day to handle a great many patients suffering from affections of the urino-genital organs, and as I always examine their rectum, I attach considerable importance to the pressure exerted upon the inserted finger by the sphincter. It is probable that the absence of these opportunities, which permit comparison between passive pederasts and normal individuals, will explain how it happens that most medico-legal experts (Tardieu among them) do not mention the results furnished by manual examination of passive pederasts.

When a catamite voluntarily submits to examination, when of his own free will he entreats the doctor's assistance and does not look upon him as representative of the authorities, when he has no reason to hide or simulate anything, then insertion of the vaseline-covered finger is easy, unimpeded and painless, if the patient is placed in the aforementioned genu-pectoral position. The finger slips through the sphincter imperceptibly and penetrates the rectal cavity, being no more gripped by this muscle than by the walls of the intestine. The sensation is quite the same as that experienced in manual exploration of the vagina of a young girl deflowered some months before. If the examination is carried still further, even the rotary movement imparted to the finger, palpitation of the prostate, digital withdrawal and reinsertion, all fail to augment pressure by the sphincter. Where the muscular atony is still more pronounced, probing with a single finger may be followed up with equal facility by bidigital exploration.

It is quite otherwise where the individual under examination is a perfectly healthy subject, and especially if he is a young man or child. In that case, the exploratory finger is clasped by the sphincter as by an elastic band. Every movement it makes, as in the operations just described, is accompanied by a new reaction due to involuntary contraction of the muscle in response to the unaccustomed irritation. As I have already pointed out, this reaction is more distinctly recognizable in children and young men. Generally, the more the individual advances in age, the less the sphincter contracts. This symptom naturally loses its diagnostic value when we are concerned with patients who have passed the age of 40, and more particularly with old men subject to piles, or who have undergone an operation intended for artificial dilatation of the sphincter.

When atony of the sphincter is highly accentuated, it gives rise to another symptom which, in my opinion, is far more pathognomonic in comparison to the others. I allude to the gaping of the anal orifice which permits the rectal walls to be seen for a depth of several centimetres. This spreading-apart of the upper layers

of the sphincter aperture may come on involuntarily
as soon as the catamite under examination assumes the
kneeling position with chest bent down, head lowered,
etc. The spontaneous opening of the anal orifice generally lasts a few moments until the gradual contraction of the muscles succeeds in closing it. But slightly
separating the nates will suffice to reproduce hiatus.
When old catamites are placed in the kneeling position
with their legs spread apart, then no matter how they
try, they do not succeed in contracting the sphincter
muscle enough to close the orifice, and the latter remains wide open throughout the examination.

This symptom has all the more value since it demands
neither special practice nor great experience on the
part of the observer. It may be discerned even in catamites who strive to dissimulate their condition, pro-
vided the examiner places them suddenly and without
warning in the kneeling position with head lowered.
During the first few moments the orifice will remain
wide open, until the subject manages to obtain contraction. This opening may likewise be observed after
operations performed upon the rectum and where the
sphincter has been sectioned or artificially dilated to
its maximum. Then again, it may be encountered at
times in decrepit old men, or very emaciated youths
who are consumptive or convalescing from dysentery,
typhoid fever, etc.

If it is possible to see the rectal walls to a certain
depth when there is involuntary gaping of the anal or-

162

ifice, or when the buttocks are held apart, then we have another symptom which has been but little noted heretofore. I have in fact often noticed breaks and longitudinal fissures in the rim of the upper layers of the sphincter and the intestinal walls. Upon separating the nates forcibly and exerting strong pressure against the sphincter, the surface of these fissures would at times discharge drops of blood. These fissures cause little pain or smarting, and heal rapidly. In non-syphilitic persons, free from piles, their origin must be attributed to passive pederasty, when there exists simultaneously a clearly marked relaxation of the sphincter.

As for the other morbid manifestations such as the development of abscesses in the perianal subcutaneous tissues, fistulas, hemorrhoidal swellings, warty excrescences, etc., their presence or absence has no diagnostic value. All the previously described morbid aspects, in connection with various kinds of neoformations like cancer, sarcoma, etc., may affect the anus and rectum of men who have never indulged in passive pederasty.

In my opinion, we should not attribute much diagnostic value to the slight prolapse of the rectal mucosa which Tardieu takes into consideration. He says on this subject that "the long mucosa of the lowest part of the rectum in the vicinity of the anal orifice forms folds and takes on the appearance of a slightly thickened coil or ring. In other cases, the folds of the mucous membrane resemble excrescences which at times attain such development that they constitute ridges somewhat similar in appearance to the labia minora of a woman's genitalia. These ridges separate when the anal orifice is stretched." I have never noted such an aspect in catamites. It does sometimes accompany recent rectal prolapse in cases having no etiologic relation whatever with pederasty.

Great relaxation of the sphincter may be revealed by relative alvine incontinence, particularly of liquid and gaseous fecal matter. This involuntary evacuation continually soils the underclothes. In young boys this condition may be the first indication by which experienced heads of institutions can recognize the vicious habits of their charges. Moreover, the skin adjoining the anus is impregnated, often irritated and even inflamed by contact with this excretion which keeps it in a perpetual state of moistness. All of this sets up such an unclean condition and so disagreeable and disgusting an odor in the affected region, that it seems impossible to imagine that their perception could arouse in the beholder any feeling other than disgust or repulsion.

CHAPTER EIGHTEEN

Modes of Contamination of Pederasts

THE most undeniable, and at the same time, the least common symptom of sodomy is the appearance of a primary syphilitic induration (hard chancre) in the immediate vicinity of the anus or rectum. It has in fact been proved that the first revelatory indication of syphilis shows up at the very site of contamination. I have often verified the presence of a hard chancre in catamites at the level where the epidermis is transformed into the mucosa, particularly on the anterior wall of the intestine and less often in the vicinity of the radial folds. When we find the hard chancre at a greater distance from the anal orifice, as for example the outer gluteal region, the perineum, the posterior face of the scrotum, it can no longer be taken as an indubitable sign of sodomy.

In view of the absence of pain from the hard chancre and the very slight discharge it produces, this primary phenomenon of syphilis may go unnoticed by the patient, or else taken for a simple fissure, a laceration, etc. It is only when the later, secondary symptoms manifest themselves, when the disease left without proper treatment degenerates into syphilitic ulcers and complications of the mucous membranes, scalp, etc., that the sick man decides to call for medical aid. But at this stage it is extremely difficult to determine the original site of the infection. The hard chancre is by this time generally healed up, leaving a difficultly perceptible scar, or it may have given place to a secondary syphilitic complication developed on the same spot (*transformatio in situ*). For example, an oozing papule may have invaded the whole anal region. When confronted with these secondary syphilitic phenomena, it is exceedingly difficult to determine exactly where the disease first showed up, that is to say the point of departure of the primary indurated ulceration. The discovery of the course and manner of the syphilitic infection remains very uncertain, because signs of secondary syphilis in the neighborhood of the anus do not in the least prove that the infection started there. It is known that secondary lesions in the perianal region may appear subsequent to various modes of contamination, for instance on the genitalia through normal coitus, or on the mouth through kissing, and so on. There is no doubt that during the later stages of syphilis the disease is very often manifested in the region of the anus and rectum, in the form of secondary ulcerations, stricture of the rectum, etc. Nevertheless, there again, localization of syphilitic lesions in the anus and rectum cannot be taken as proof that the infection started out from there. That is why only the actual presence of an undeniable primary syphilitic induration in the rectum or immediate vicinity of the anus may be considered as patent proof of sodomy.

You may wonder if it is not really possible for syphilitic infection to be brought about through the anus by some way other than sodomy. Evidently we cannot dispute this point theoretically. But if we consider facts only, I may say that all hard chancres of the rectum which I have observed till now—and they are very many—came from sodomy. I know but one case where a chancre showed up at the level of an operated fistula, either because the surgeon had not taken the necessary precautions, or through the fault of the assistant entrusted with renewing the dressings.

An acquired pederast, if he gets the disease, (and a mercenary catamite even more so) generally tries to explain the contamination by maintaining that he had gone to the toilet right after a person afflicted with syphilis, or else that he had sat down in a bath-tub which a syphilitic had just gotten out of, or that he had by mistake applied a dressing which belonged to a syphilitic. These fabrications and others make it easier for the patient to admit his diseased condition, but they are not at all plausible, for it is not by these procedures that the syphilitic virus may go through the sphincter and attack the rectal mucosa. It usually happens that when the patient's confidence has been won at the end of a certain time, he will make new confessions which establish the true manner of infection.

But while a primary syphilitic induration of the anus or rectum constitutes evident proof of sodomy, it is not at all the same with the presence of a chancroid, or soft chancre, in the same region. It is extremely rare for a soft chancre to develop in the anus as a result of sodomy. We do frequently meet with ulcerations of this nature of the periphery of the anus, but they are consequent upon other causes. This is partly due to the fact that the chancroid usually appears not as a solitary complication, but rather in the company of other lesions of the same character, whence the existence of pain and copious supuration. For one thing, the pain and multiplicity of ulcerations prevent the patient from ignoring his condition, and then again, they make the practice of sodomy extremely difficult. Yet there are undoubtedly exceptions.

At the beginning of the past school term, I had to treat a young catamite, 14 years of age, at the Imperial Academy of Medicine. The boy was suffering from an enormous phagedenic chancroid of the rectum. The ulceration occupied the whole vicinity of the anus and penetrated into the rectum to a height of 4 centimeters, thus causing the patient terrible pains every time he defecated. The lesion had its point of departure in a fissure situated at the boundary between the epidermis and rectal mucosa, and from there it had invaded the whole region surrounding the anus, without being accompanied by any soft chancre of the genitals or other parts of the body.

But I must repeat, such observations are exceptions. Soft chancre most often appear in the anus simultaneously with identical ulcerations of the genital organs, and have their origin in auto-inoculation at the level of the radial folds. When the pus issuing from a soft chancre reaches the level of the cutaneous surface where the epidermis is eroded or lacerated, then the latter becomes readily inoculated and leads to formation of a new chancroid. It is precisely this auto-inoculation with pus from a soft chancre which serves to explain the multiplicity of these ulcerations on the patient, as well as their appearance on the anus following an infection originally seated in the genital organs.

That is why in women who have contracted soft chancre on the outer genitalia during coitus, when the pus starts to flow and passes their very short perineum, if it reaches the radial folds of the anus and encounters some accidental laceration or fissure, then inoculation sets in at once. It has been noticed in women treated at the Kalinkin Hospital that soft chancre of the anal region is a matter of daily observation. Yet in these cases sodomy is, of course, quite outside the question. The frequency of these chancroids of the anus is especially great among women who are not prostitutes and therefore not submitted by the police to regular medical inspection. For this reason they may go without appropriate treatment for a long time before their admission to the hospital. Attention may be called here to the fact that in Saint Petersburg sodomy is extremely rare amongst women, even prostitutes.

In men, the discharge of pus from soft chancres of the penis is usually checked in its descent towards the anus by the scrotum, and therefore chancroids of the anal region are much less common in them than in women. Nevertheless, if the man scratches his anus with a finger polluted by venereal pus, at the time a dressing is being made, then he may sometimes induce auto-inoculation of the radial folds. It may happen that the original soft chancres situated on the genitalia will be healed while those on the anus still persist, because of their unfavorable location from the point of view of cleanliness and facility of dressing. Consequently, when chancroids are discovered on the radial folds, care must be taken to determine by thorough examination whether their origin may not be attributed to identical lesions previously situated on the genital parts. We see, therefore, that a soft chancre can only in very exceptional cases be taken as evidence of sodomy, and even then it must have started in the rectum, without previous or simultaneous lesions of the same nature on the sexual organs.

Gonorrhea of the rectum in consequence of sodomy is of still greater rarity. I have only twice had occasion to observe genuine acute gonorrhea of the rectum, and both times it was in young mercenary catamites, bath-house boys aged 15 and 17. No doubt the appearance of rectal gonorrhea in a young subject is almost conclusive proof, except that we must know how to distinguish gonorrhea from the moist exudation and catarrh brought on by worms. This is actually not very difficult. But what is much more so is to differentiate between gonorrhea and the traumatic irritation of the rectum noticeable in onanists who introduce various objects into the anus. These may begin with pencils and go on to glasses and bottles.[1] In adult subjects, particularly in old men suffering from chronic piles, fistulas, prolapse of the rectum or rectal catarrh, we may often observe a copious discharge of pus which simulates that of gonorrhea. That is why it is only in young subjects, showing no symptom of other rectal affections, that purulent catarrh of this organ may be considered as evidence of sodomy.

Former observers like Zacchias, for example, recognized the production of verrucose excrescences (called condylomas or more accurately papillomas) in the anal region as sure signs of sodomy. Even the Latin satirists make allusion to the "combs" and "knobs" about

---

1. Moraud, Collection de plusieurs observations singulières sur des corps étrangers, les uns appliqués aux parties naturelles, d'autres insinués dans la vessie et d'autres dans le fondement. *Mémoires de l'Académie Royale de Chirurgie*, 1757, tome III, p.260.

the anus as proof of sodomy. Thus Juvenal says in one
of his most celebrated poems:

"Sed podice laevi
Caeduntur tumidae, medico ridente, mariscae."

It is quite true that I have had occasion to observe the
formation of warty excrescences in confirmed catamites, especially mercenary ones, who often practice
sodomy several times a day. These excrescences are
situated on the rim of the anal orifice, the radial cutaneous folds and even on the walls of the rectum. But
these protrusions may be seen even more frequently
where there has been no sodomy. These papillomas are
observable in children having catarrhal inflammation
of the rectum as a result of the presence of worms.
Then again, we may encounter them in adults suffering from piles, or in old men having prurigo of the anus. Sometimes it is quite impossible to discover the
cause for the continued growth of such papillomas in
the vicinity of the anus. We may sum up by saying that
the presence of verrucose protuberances of the anus
can not be considered by itself as a sign of sodomy,
and that it is only when associated with other characteristic deformations that these protrusions may serve
partly to confirm the existence of sodomistic habits.
Now there remains to be mentioned a more particular
symptom, first described by Casper and particularly
stressed by him. That is a peculiar conical indentation
of the buttocks towards the anus. Casper says: "A pos-

terior of this sort does not present the usual two hemispheres, but the inner face is leveled out to within 1½ to 2 inches of the anus, with the result that there is a certain indentation between the nates, a cone-shaped cavity. This cavity is almost constantly encountered in habitual passive pederasts."

In my opinion, the complete or incomplete juxtaposition of the nates, as well as the greater or lesser convexity of their inner faces, depend above all upon their tension, the age of the subject examined, his position during the examination, the contraction or relaxation of the muscles, and least of all upon passive pederasty. Thus, in accordance with the different positions we make the examined subject assume, we at one moment observe the conoidal depression, while at the next instant it will have disappeared. Even the etiology ascribed to this symptom is incorrect. According to Casper, the inner surface of the buttocks gets flattened out through the tension produced by rectal intromission. But in reality nothing of the sort takes place, because in order to facilitate this intromission the nates are always forced apart with the hands, and in this way they are not subjected to any pressure by the penis. Casper maintains that this sign indicated by him is one of the most conclusive of all the uncertain symptoms of passive pederasty. It appears to me more in line with the truth to reverse Casper's assertion and say that the conoidal depression between the buttocks is the least conclusive of all the sure signs of passive pederasty.

CHAPTER NINETEEN

Cases of Sodomistic
Rape--Causes

Now that we have reviewed the signs of habitual pederasty, we shall draw attention to the symptoms discovered in examining cases where the practice of
sodomy is of quite recent date. All observations of this
nature belong essentially in the category of sodomistic
rape. This act is committed by impulsive pederasts
during a fit, by old men in a seizure of senile dementia, or even by congenital active pederasts suffering
from an advanced stage of psychic degeneration. In
fact it is only when the intelligence has fallen quite low,
or when the pederast is under the influence of some
well-defined psychic disturbance, that the act of sodomy is performed unexpectedly and with a certain a-
mount of violence. In the great majority of cases, the
catamite is gradually habituated to his functions.
Sometimes months are spent in preliminary training
so that by the time the act is fully consummated, it is

not rare for the catamite to possess the distinctive signs of sodomy: anal infundibulum, relaxation of the sphincter, and other characteristic phenomena.

We must therefore give our attention now to the signs revealed by sodomy recently practiced on an unprepared subject, in other words to the crime called sodomistic rape. It would be more correct to call it "sodomy accompanied by violence", because real rape, the performance of the complete act from start to finish and against the catamite's will, is impossible. Certainly there are cases where little children aged two or three have been forced to submit to sodomy, either because the pedicator had the assistance of several other persons, or because the child involved was in a state of unconsciousness. But these cases are rare exceptions. Most usually the overtures to the act are readily accepted, and only occasionally is the act itself concluded by the use of a certain amount of violence.

A subject who has been forced this way (generally a boy or young man) will complain for a few days following the act of a painful sensation during defecation, and of aches when he sits down on a hard seat. His walk is somewhat modified, the legs being kept farther apart than usual. Then the pain subsides gradually and gives way to itching. Exploration of the anus discloses inflamed redness of the adjoining skin, swelling, and numerous slight excoriations of the rectal mucosa. Other slighter excoriations will be found on the periphery and outer epidermis, where they are accompanied by ecchymotic spots. Often, there flows from the anal orifice a purulent-looking discharge, mixed with blood. Touching the rectum is painful, because it provokes contraction of the levator and sphincter muscles.

It is only the use of considerable violence, by a man of very large parts, that could lead to relaxation of the sphincter during these first days, whether through extraordinary distension or actual tearing of the flesh. In that event, another symptom would supervene: incontinence of fecal matter and involuntary breaking of wind. Lastly, when violence has been pushed to the utmost extremes, the subcutaneous tissues of the anal periphery may be inflamed under the influence of the severe traumatism, and give rise to abscesses or consecutive fistulas.

Where the violence has been very great, we may also observe certain other lesions in the victim, particularly in the region of the genital organs. It is even possible from their extent to guess at the amount of force brought to the consummation of the act. Quite often we may note edema of the prepuce (whose border may show fissures), rupture of the frenum, erosions of the scrotum and perineum. The latter may likewise be the site of hemal extravasation. In a case reported by Tardieu, the whole skin of the penis, from the very root, was torn away by torsion and turned inside out like the finger of a glove.[1] In another case, concluded by

1. Tardieu, *loc. cit.*, p.267.

murder of the victim, it was verified that the scrotum was highly edematized and that there had been copious hemorrhage. In a third case, where two men had perpetrated sodomistic rape upon a three-year old child, after having killed it in most barbarous fashion, deep traces of bites were found on the unfortunate victim's corpse, and there were lacerations made with the nails at the root of the penis and on the scrotum. Casper likewise reports a case of sodomistic violation upon a little boy aged five. Here the act was accompanied by attempts to strangle the victim. The child's prepuce was torn so badly that the subcutaneous tissues were exposed down to the corpora cavernosa.[1] Still graver assaults upon the genital organs were noted in the case described by Dr. Marquisi.[2]

The signs we have described are attenuated by every passing day. They begin to disappear, lose their significance, and it becomes almost impossible to detect them two or three months after the assault, save in exceptional cases, as for example when there has been syphilitic infection. I have reasons, based upon observation, which lead me to believe that sodomy practiced once or twice with a certain amount of violence upon a child of 10 or 11 would, at the end of two or three months, leave no visible trace of deformation in the anus or rectum. Therefore I do not accord as much cre-

---

1. Mierzejewski, *loc. cit.,* p.228
2. Giraldès et P. Horteloup Sur un cas de meurtre avec viol sodomitique, *Annales d'hygiène et de médecine légale.* 2e série, tome XLI, p.419.

dence as Dr. Espallac[1] to the story of a girl of 12 who maintained that she had but twice submitted to sodomy, yet two months afterwards, the slightest separation of her nates brought on relaxation of the sphincter and gaping of the anal orifice.

The set of facts which we have developed gives convincing proof that habitual passive pederasty, and recent or accidental pederasty even more so, may be recognized upon examination by means of indubitable, objective signs. Another question comes up, and that is to know whether the previously described deformations of the anus, rectum, and genital organs, perceptible upon examination, may be taken as sufficiently conclusive for recognition of all cases of passive pederasty. We shall study this point subsequently, and for the time being shall consider whether there are signs of active pederasty.

Tardieu is the only observer who answers in the affirmative. In his opinion, which he supports by 133 cases, the penis of the active pederast presents certain deviations from the normal type. This conclusion may be allowed in certain cases. Tardieu finds that individuals who make an habitual practice of active pederasty have an exceedingly slender, underdeveloped penis with a glans of small size, and that the penis diminishes in volume from the root towards the distal end, so as to resemble somewhat the penis of a dog. In rare

---

1. Tardieu, *loc. cit.*, p. 227.

instances, the penis is thicker than usual, and then the glans alone tapers sharply, while the trunk is twisted about its axis, so that the urethral meatus may be situated sidewise or present a lateral slit. In order to explain this deformation, and especially the tapering from the glans plus the torsion of the trunk, Tardieu invokes the pressure of the sphincter and the violent effort necessary for the act.

The inadequacy of Tardieu's explanation is evident. The principal sign he indicates, consisting of the smallness and slenderness of the whole organ including the glans, is not at all a consequence of pederasty. Besides, it is not the explanation which is important, but the fact itself. Now, it appears to me that Tardieu's observation is correct up to a certain point, but that he has too hastily drawn conclusions from isolated cases, with the result that his explanation is quite erroneous. From my personal studies I may affirm that the majority of active pederasts who freely practice their vice present no appreciable deformation of the penis such as would permit one to guess their vicious bent. All acquired pederasts, mercenary active pederasts, old men in a state of morbid degeneration, in short, the largest part of active pederasts show no difference whatever of their genitals from those of normal individuals.

Of course there may be relatively rare cases where congenital active pederasts present visible deviations in the development of their sex organs. I have already pointed out that this form of pederasty is in many instances produced by a much more advanced degree of degeneration than we commonly encounter in passive pederasts. That is why thorough examination in such cases will usually disclose evident marks of arrested development, among which we may find defective or irregular constitution of the sexual parts. In this sense Tardieu's observation is correct.

Moreover, if we consider the general fact that the study of physical signs of degeneration is still in its infancy, then naturally we must not neglect any of them, especially when the sign is as plain as defective or irregular development of the genitals. For instance, out of four active pederasts whom I know at the present time, there are two whose penis is remarkably slender, with tapering glans. The third has his member slightly inclined to one side as a result of a symmetric development of the corpora cavernosa, and because of equally defective conformation of the spongy tissues along the urethra, the glans is so directed that the meatus is not vertical, but oblique. The fourth is afflicted with congenital phimosis and atrophy of one of the testicles, although the general appearance and volume of the penis seem normal. In all four, aside from the aforementioned deviations, one may observe other signs clearly indicative of psycho-physical degeneration.

It is evidently impossible to number an individual amongst pederasts just because he shows such deformations of the sexual parts as we have just described.

Etiology of Sexual Abnormality

The same aspects may be met with in persons of normal sex functions. But when it is a confirmed pederast who bears these anomalies, we almost invariably have before us a case of perversion that is not acquired, but congenital. It must also be obvious that visual examination of the sexual parts and of the body in general furnishes no true sign upon which we may base a proof of active pederasty, even with fair certainty. Nevertheless, any development of the sexual parts which deviates from the normal type in pederasts seems to designate congenital perversion of the procreative instinct. It is not possible to diagnose pederasty in general by the signs accurately described by Tardieu, but thanks to them we can with certainty determine the etiology of the sexual abnormality in pederasts.

CHAPTER TWENTY

Establishing Nature of Inversion

W E have now reviewed all the known signs of pederasty. Are they sufficient, if not in all cases, then at least in the majority of cases, to prove the existence of pederasty? Unfortunately, it does not work out that way. We have just seen that in active pederasts there is no distinctive sign which permits recognizing them upon examination. And if we leave them out, we have to admit that it is also very difficult to diagnose all passive pederasts as such. Pederasty, in the broadest sense of the word, is not always manifested in the form of sodomy. We called attention to this previously. Active pederasts who do not go in for actual sodomy, but practice intromission *inter femora,* or fellation, will because of this very fact present no deformation of the anus, rectum or genital organs. Passive pederasty, too, when it begins to be practiced by a demented old man, even if he is afflicted with piles, will leave no characteristic trace in the anal region. These signs will also be lacking in periodic pederasts who perform the act only at long intervals, during which the deformed parts have ample time to return to their normal state.

But even in the limited number of cases where the existing physical signs do reveal sodomy, are these sufficient to settle the question of primary importance, that is, do we have to do with an hereditary taint or a vicious habit? Certainly not! The signs thus far noted in pederasts throw no light on the question of whether the examined individual is a mercenary catamite who earns money in this shameful way, or whether he is a subject suffering from a disease whose symptoms are manifested in the form of sexual perversion. Nor do these signs indicate whether or not the subject is an unfortunate of retarded development, who from birth on has been deprived of the faculty of having normal sex relations. To sum up, we may say that deformations of the anus, rectum or genital parts, taken by themselves, leave the main question in abeyance by not establishing the nature of the inversion.

The solution of this important problem demands an entirely different method of investigation. When we are concerned with a young man, we must apply our efforts toward determining whether he is sane or psychopathic, by means of careful study of his heredity, physical degeneration or psychic aberrations, etc. If the subject is found sane, then signs of pederasty denote an acquired pederast. If the subject is a psychopath, it is highly probable that his vice was innate. When the young man alternately accepts the passive and active roles, and can concurrently have intercourse with women, then it is demonstrated that the perversion of the sex instinct is acquired. The congenital form, on the other hand, is in the vast majority of cases (particularly in young men) manifested by exclusive inclination towards passive pederasty and incapacity for relations with women. The rare cases of congenital active pederasty, always accompanied by well-defined psychic anomalies, also permit us at times to ascertain abnormal development of the genitals. Subjects of this category are in general not only deprived of the power to perform coitus with women, but also feel real hatred for them.

When an adult is submitted to examination, the question becomes much more complicated. There it is necessary to collect all the facts on heredity, the anamnesis of early life, and step by step to follow the patient's life to the present time, with special attention to the age of puberty. These data combined with thorough study of the subject's physical and psychic peculiarities will then assist us in our incumbent task of deciding whether we have to do with a case of congenital or acquired sex perversion. In the first instance, as soon as we know the time and conditions under which the vice began, the frequency and uniformity of the act, etc., we can establish whether or not the examined subject belongs to the most dangerous, yet least punishable, class of inverts, the periodic pederasts. When the existence of a congenital sexual perversion is contra-indicated by well-established facts, it is necessary to determine whether the observed phenomenon is a symptom of incipient progressive paralysis, or lastly whether it is a premonitory sign of senile dementia. It is only after eliminating the above-mentioned status, and in basing our conclusions on facts deduced from painstaking study and observation, that we are justified in asserting the probable existence of depravation, absolute license, voluntary and premeditated, together with moral responsibility in the individual under examination.

CHAPTER TWENTY-ONE

Age, Pederasty, Punishments

THE solution of these questions meets with the greatest difficulties when we have to do with aged men. In such instances the most arduous task is recognizing whether inversion is a symptom of incipient senile dementia or really a vice arising from the perpetual quest for new means to revive the dying sexual potency. The gradual decline of the mental faculties and attenuation of feelings escape the attention of the sick man's friends and even strangers, until they approach the last stages. The mental debility passes quite imperceptibly from what we ordinarily call feeblemindedness to complete collapse of the intellectual faculties.

A real imbecile cannot grasp the sense of a syllogism in its entirety. Each premise is for him an idea apart, and it is beyond his comprehension to connect it with the preceding one or the one that follows, to fix them in his memory or draw conclusions from them. In this

clearly defined form imbecility makes for easy diagnosis. But if we go a few grades higher in the scale, we
encounter an individual able to reason, draw conclusions, associate several consecutive ideas, but who does
not have the faculty for conceiving a thing in its general relationships, for giving up a chain of ideas once
he has adopted them, or for examining a subject from
different points of view. There is but a step from this
mental debility to complete blotting out of the mind.
The patient may treat a subject in a general sort of
way, but with continual loss of the main idea, and he
becomes confused by the addition of details and ac-
cessories to the point of losing the continuity. As a result he never reaches any logical conclusion.

The habit of empty talk, which sounds fairly logical,
and sometimes witty, constitutes one of the commonest
signs of the beginnings of the intellectual decay due to
age, or arising in individuals exhausted by all sorts of
excesses. It quite often happens that this same symptom is combined with the sort of mental poverty im-
plied when people say a man is of "average intelligence". Absence of the full power of reasoning, insufficiency of critical faculties, inaptitude for distinguishing what is important from what is unimportant,
lack of independence in the effort to discover the cause
and nature of things, a tendency to look at things from
one side only, loss of creative power and capacity for
original thinking, these are just so many tangible
symptoms which disclose various degrees of mental

impoverishment and decay. One must have been acquainted with the patient for a long time to set up a firm basis for comparison between his normal intellectual activity in the past, and his present, pathologically depressed mental power. And these mental faculties do not only consist of the thinking and creative processes. Before any conclusion may be arrived at, one must also take into consideration the patient's receptivity to external impressions, their fixation in the realm of consciousness, his memory, faculty for comprehension, logic, feelings.

It is even more difficult to recognize an enfeeblement of the senses, for there we have no outward sign of the loss of sensitivity. This is not less true in the case of hyperaesthesia which reveals not the intensity of sensitivity but its manner of expression. It is easy to understand that where the intelligence has declined and the senses have become enfeebled, the two most potent means of resistance against the passions become inoperative. (Do we not recognize the degree of virtue a man attains by his intelligence and the measure of his sensitivity?) To these two factors constituting the dominant note in the collective character of the feebleminded, there is later added increased lust, whose influence at times makes the subject guilty of a whole series of criminal acts. In fact, when it is demonstrated that the individual in question has previously enjoyed the use of normal sex functions, that these have gradually diminished, disappeared finally, but reappeared at certain intervals with new vigor though in perverted fashion, then there can be no doubt that we are confronted with a case of incipient senile dementia. Above all, sex desires out of all keeping with the subject's age are early symptoms of a morbid state in process of evolving.

The depraved individual seeks a new procedure for intensifying his erethism, by modifying the manner and means of performing the sex act, as well as its preparation. Accordingly, the manifestation of the sex instinct is generally somewhat different in the two cases. The depraved individual employs all accessible means which may help to increase his desires. Sight, touch, hearing, smell, even taste, and sometimes all the senses one after the other, are excited to a certain degree to bring the erethism to its maximum intensity. It is under the influence of these excitations that passive pederasty makes its appearance as an accidental, accessory phenomenon, as a new stimulant which may serve to augment the erethism, which then finds satisfaction in normal intercourse with a woman. Sometimes such subjects add the use of external and internal stimulants, the reading of pornographic works, etc. Despite the apparent insatiability of his desires, the depraved individual is occasionally capable of regaining self-control, and may then show himself to be a model husband, a stern judge who frowns upon vice.

On the other hand, in authentic cases of senile dementia, the patient does not seek excitation. Always incapable of dissimilating his sensual desires, he leads conversations around to the subject of sexual relations, becomes shameless, and even indulges in indecent gestures. And this is all aimed not at self-excitation, but at gratification of the incessantly growing sexual erethism that torments him. For the same reason, he rejects normal intercourse with women, because they are unable to sate his morbid desires. Then again, by passing from women to little girls and infants, and not finding sufficient gratification, he may become tranformed into an active pederast. Still later, in the midst of all the different means to which he resorts to satisfy his lusts, there may gradually develop an exacerbated need for inflicting physical suffering upon his victims. Shrieks, moans, convulsive movements come to have greater effect on the patient than the organ of voluptuous pleasure, and consequently he strives to find complete gratification in this direction. Under the influence of this feeling he begins by biting and scratching, then goes on to cutting and beheading, prey that he is to the exclusive desire to satisfy his constantly growing morbid lusts by any possible means. The foregoing description shows how much the nature and expression of the sexual drive in an individual merely depraved differ from the insatiable lust of a feebleminded old man and his desperate efforts to stop the pathologic irritation of his sexual sense.

In the latter, there are numerous instances where the sexual desire is accompanied by inhibitive feelings which in a healthy individual would suffice to stifle the desire. Such feelings are malice, rage, an urge to make the victim suffer, to witness the torture, to hear the cries, to realize plainly that the victim is meeting a horrible death. A diseased old man of this kind will at times lavish caresses on his victim at the very moment he is tearing apart the disemboweled body from which the blood is streaming. His passion becomes exalted, and he utters terrible threats at the very moment when he performs the act of coitus.

The depraved individual, on the contrary, attaches the greatest importance to external conditions, seeking to avoid and ward off painful feelings. He strives to concentrate on the pleasures of voluptuousness, and is consequently finicky, capricious, extra-fastidious, whereas the feebleminded old man will perform the sex act under most any conditions, sometimes satisfying his tastes in the most scandalous, disgusting manner. The depraved subject will make his victim neat and clean, will wash him and perfume him with pleasant odors, comb him and dress him according to his fancy, while the diseased old man will violate a dirty, ragged little tramp in some stinking stable.

But however different the forms assumed by the phenomena revealing senile dementia, we must consider that there are numerous ill-defined intermediate stages where it is impossible to determine where vice ends and disease begins. In general, I believe it highly probable that disease exists when we detect overwrought sex desires combined with instincts of cruelty, an urge to make the victim suffer at the time of the orgasm, an urge to inflict bruises and wounds. Of course it is only the continuity of cruelty during the sex-act that is characteristic. It is not at all the same with accidental bites, blows or wounds which may be inflicted by a hot-blooded subject at the peak of venereal excitement or in a moment of drunkenness.

I have but briefly indicated the conditions which may more or less settle the question, in a case of inversion, as to whether we are dealing with a vice of congenital development or a vicious habit that has been acquired, whether there is deep-rooted depravity or nervous disease. This rapid review tends to show how much this sort of individual requires thorough-going examination, the care to be taken in tracing the minutest details of his life, of taking into account the possible influence of education, example, intercurrent maladies, etc. We must consider the slightest details in the development and activity of his sex instinct, the mental and emotional world he lives in, as well as his social and family environment. We must obtain full information as to the state of health, character and habits of the patient's parents, and all his blood relations. In short, we must procure as much data as possible upon his heredity, environment and other possible factors for degeneration. It is only then that we will be able with fair certainty to determine what type of sex perversion confronts us, and to disclose the cause of the aberration, so far as our present knowledge will permit.

If each medico-legal case of inversion is treated this way, it is easy to see what a mass of details must be collected for the investigation, and what a difficult, complex task devolves upon the medical expert. I believe, therefore, that if the facts I have just set forth have sufficient value as proof, then in the future, inversion will no longer be attributed exclusively to license and depravity, and the examination will not be confined to the subject's anus and genitals. I know very well that there is nothing more prejudicial to the man afflicted with a mental disorder and who commits crimes when in a state of aberration than the false philanthropy and mercenary eloquence which seek to generalize the principal of irresponsibility, and substitute a wholly fabricated mental aberration for real, unquestionable guilt. In pursuing this study it has been far from my intention to supply vice with a weapon against the law.

CHAPTER TWENTY-TWO

Sexual Physiology in Jurisprudence

UNTIL now, studies of sexual deviations have paid too little attention to hereditary taints and to disease. My aim was mainly to emphasize the addition of these factors to the study of the subject under examination. Therefore I have spoken as little as possible about moral depravation (although I am far from underrating the importance of vice as a factor), because I merely wanted to arrive at establishing its distinction from those pathologic complications which make it so difficult a task to estimate impartially the extent of moral decay in a really depraved individual.

The association of disease with vice always diminishes the latter's importance. Can we for example compare the gradual corruption of a child, who is led step by step to indulge in vice, with the gross, brutal performance of sodomistic rape? In the first case we find neither threats nor violence. Everything takes place smoothly, and gradually develops so as to attain the goal as if spontaneously. Vice usually surrounds itself with such precautions that it rarely ends up in the prisoner's dock, and still more rarely has to undergo punishment. In the other case, not only is an immoral act perpetrated, but the victim's sense of decency is utterly outraged, his will overcome and his physical being subjected to violence. If we invoke the same impulsive origin in both instances, there is no doubt that vicious education of a subject should be considered a slight offense in comparison with rape by force. But in reality, specially training a subject in vice is the most abominable expression of combined depravity, whereas pederastic rape is most often a manifestation of senile dementia. When we are confronted with morbid symptoms, even the wildest immorality fades away, and our right to punish it diminishes quite as much. The more clearly and precisely we can determine the question of acquired vice, the more evident become even mild offenses against decency, and the justness of punishing them. Otherwise, these might be included in the mass of pathologic actions and escape castigation.

It is naturally beyond the present power of science to distinguish in all cases between vice and disease. We are just as little able to distinguish at all times between crime and psychosis. Maudsley says that "between crime and insanity there exists a border zone where we encounter on one side a small part of insanity and a large proportion of crime, while on the other side we find a slight admixture of crime and a great measure of insanity." This applies admirably to the relationship between vice and disease. Undoubtedly there is a transitional terrain between the two, a boundary zone where it is difficult, if not altogether impossible, to determine the proportion of intentional, premeditated vice and that of hereditary predisposition.

If we leave out the obscure cases, the exceptional ones that cannot be decided, we have at our disposal a scientific basis for establishing a distinction between vice and disease. And when we have attained greater perfection in this field of knowledge, I believe that this scientific basis will give practical results of greater utility than the numerous treatises founded on principles enunciated in defense of morality and sobriety. When we have definitely recognized a disease, it will be difficult for anyone to imitate its symptoms, especially if it becomes common knowledge that certain manifestations of this malady always indicate an abnormal condition of the nervous centres and an enfeeblement of the mind.

At the present time not only does vice seem seductive to most individuals because of the intensity, novelty or diversity of the sensations it excites, but it also gives the sexual libertine a certain air of epicureanism, originality, and a reputation for vice and superiority over other beings who appear less highly developed than he, but who are really more moral and more temperate. There is an idea prevalent in society that once the senses are sated with ordinary enjoyments, they tend towards refinements of license, and seek sexual gratification in more subtle, more intensified pleasures. This seemingly inventive genius of vice usually causes it to be supposed that there is actually something better and completer than the ordinary way of satisfying the sex instinct. Consequently, the conviction of having vicious propensities and sexual depravity raises certain ignorant, weak-minded individuals in their own esteem and in that of the persons about them. This attractive aspect of vice which favors imitation of morbid depravity must lose its charm as soon as it is known that vice in its more violent manifestations is symptomatic of a pathologic state which is accompanied by a certain blunting, and not a sharpening, of sensations, together with imperfect balance of the nervous system. It is thus evident that vice is far from tending towards perfection, and eminently favorable to the evolution of mental disorders and weakening of the mind.

In this respect, the law-courts can do a highly important service to society by broadcasting a set of sound opinions. I am completely in accord with Michelet when he says: "Jurisprudence must become a medical science, based upon physiology, whose aim will be to determine the amount of influence that unavoidable, subconscious impulses may have upon voluntary acts."

I am convinced that only the combined efforts of physicians and jurists, research-workers and philosophers, will succeed in discovering the causes for these impulses and their expression in acts, in tracing the limits between the normal physiology and the pathology of the living being, and finally furnish a firm basis for the perfecting of healthy individuals, the correction of those with morbid tendencies, and the cure of beings afflicted with disease.

Bibliography of Important Works Treating with Inversion and Pederasty

ADAM, PAUL. La Mésaventure, *Revue Indépendante,* 1888.

ALBERT, DR. Friedrich's Blätter, 1859, III, p. 77.

ALCIPHRON. Letters.

ALCAEUS. Ganymedes.

ANJEL. Ueber eigenthümliche Anfälle perverser Sexualerregung, *Arch. f. Psych., Bd.* XV. Heft 2.

ANONYMOUS. Entgegnung auf: Hoche: Zur Frage der forensischen Beurteilung sexueller Vergehen. Mendels Neurolog. Centralblatt 15 Januar 1896 in Friedrich's Blätter für gerichtliche Medizin. Heft II, Nov. and Dec. 1896.

ANONYMOUS. Aus dem dunkelsten Berlin: Die männliche Prostitution. Berlin 1897 von K. v. K. Im "Reporter." III. Welt-Blatt, Verlag von Kresse, Lenz & Co. Jahrgang III. N° 14.

ANONYMOUS. Die Sinnenlust und ihre Opfer, Berlin, 1869.

— Das Paradoxe der Venus Urania, Berlin, 1869.

ANONYMOUS. Entgegnung auf Hüpeden:
Bemerkungen zu Krafft-Ebings:
Der Konträrsexuale vor dem Strafrichter, in *Stengleins Gerichtssaal,* vol. LI, Fasc. 5 and 6.

— Noch ein Wort zu Krafft-Ebings:
Der Konträrsexuale vor dem Straf-
richter in *Gerichtssaal,* vol. LII,
Fasc. 5.

ANONYMOUS. Enthüllungen über Leben
und Lehren der Katholischen Geistlichkeit.
Sondershausen bei G. Neus, 1862.

ANONYMOUS. Entwurf eines Strafgesetzbuches für das Königreich Hannover. Art.
273, p. 156.

ANONYMOUS. Ist "freie Liebe" Sittenlos-
igkeit? Leipzig, Max Spohr.

ANONYMOUS. Entgegnung auf: Högel:
Die Verkehrtheit des Geschlechtstriebes im
Strafrecht-Gerichtssaal. Vol. LIII, Fasc. 1
and 2 in *Gerichtssaal,* Vol. LIII, Fasc. 6.

ANONYMOUS. Paragraph 175 und die
Urningsliebe. *Zeitschrift für die gesamte Stra-
frechtswissenschaft,* v. List. vol. XII, Fasc. 3.

ANONYMOUS. Der Konträrsexualismus in
Bezug auf Ehe und Frauenfrage. Leipzig, von
Max Spohr, ed[r].

ANONYMOUS. Die Berliner Prostitution,
Von einem Polizeibeamten. Berlin, 1847.

ANONYMOUS. Ein Weib? Psychologisch-
biographische Studie über eine Konträrsexu-
elle. Leipzig, Max Spohr.

ANTIPHANES. Ganymedes.

— Päderastes.

ARGIS, HENRI d'. Sodome. Paris, Piaget,
1888.

— Gomorrhe.

ARREAT, L. Sexualité et altruisme, *Revue philosophique, Paris,* Dec. 1886.

ARRUFAT, J. Essai sur un mode d'évolution de l'instinct sexuel, Lyon, Paris, 1893.

ATHENAEUS. The Philosophers' Banquet.

AURELIUS. Rubi. Novelle, Berlin, 1879.

BAFFO, GIORGIO. Poésies complètes de Giorgio Baffo en dialecte vénitien, littéralement traduites pour la première fois, avec le texte en regard. Paris, Liseux, 1884, 3 vol.

BAHR, HERM. Die Mutter.

BALL, DR. La Folie érotique.

BALZAC, HONORÉ DE. La Fille aux yeux d'or.

BARBEZ, HENRY. Obsession avec conscience, aberration du sens génital. *Gazette hebdomad. de médecine et de chirurgie,* 2ᵉ série, t. XXIII. Paris, 1890.

BAUER, HENRY. Chronique sur l'affaire Oscar Wilde, *Écho de Paris,* 3 août 1895.

BECCADELLI, ANTONIUS PANOR-MITA. Hermaphroditus, Cobourg, 1824.

BECCARIA. L'Attica Venere, Dei delitti e delle pene. Harlem and Paris, 1766.

BELOT, ADOLPHE. La bouche de Madame X.
— Mˡˡᵉ Giraud, ma femme.

BÉRAUD. Les filles publiques de Paris et la police qui les régit. 1839.

BERNHARDI, W. Der Uranismus. Lösung eines mehrtausendjährigen Rätsels. Berlin, 1882.

BERNHARDY. Griechische Litteraturgeschichte, I, 42.

BERNSTEIN. Aus Akten eines Sensationsprozesses.

— Die Beurteilung des Widernormalen Geschlechtsverkehrs. *Neue Zeit.,* 1894-1895; 32 and 34.

BETHGE, HANS. Die stillen Inseln. Ein Gedichtbuch. Berlin, 1898.

BIRKET, J. Case in which persistent priapism, etc. *The Lancet,* 1867, vol. I, p. 207.

BIRNBACHER. Ein Fall von konträrer Sexualempfindung vor dem Strafgericht. *Friedrich's Blätter für gerichtliche Medizin.* Nürnberg, 1894, 42, 1.

BLANC, E. LISA WEISE. Ein Stimmungsmensch. Novelle, *Berliner Tageblatt,* April 1897.

BLEULER. Besprechung von Molls Buch: "Die konträre Sexualempfindung". *Münchner medizinische Wochenschrift,* 1892, n° 11.

BLONDEAU, NICOLAS. Dictionnaire érotique latin-français, précédé d'un Essai sur la langue érotique, par le traducteur du "Manuel d'Erotologie" de Forberg. Paris, Liseux, 1885.

BLUMENSTOCK. Konträre Sexualempfindung. Realencyclopädie der ges. Heilkunde. 2 Aufl. Vol. VI, 1885.

BLUMER ALDER. A case of perverted sexual instinct, *American Journ. of Insanity,* July, 1882.

BLUMRÖDER. Ueber Lust und Schmerz, Friedreich's Magazin für Seelenheilkunde. 1830, II.

BOETTICHER, KARL. Eros und die Erkenntniss bei Plato. Berlin, 1894.

BONNETAIN, PAUL. Charlot s'amuse.

— L'Opium.

BORDIER. Étude anthropologique sur une série de crânes d'assassins, *Revue d'Anthropologie,* 1879.

BÖTTIGER, CARL AUGUST. Sabina II, 27. Leipzig, 1813.

BOUHOURS, R. P. Sentiments des Jésuites touchant le péché philosophique.

BOURGES, ÉLÉMIR. Le crépuscule des dieux.

BOUVIER. Manuel des confesseurs.

BRIERRE DE BOISMONT. Remarques médico-légales sur la perversion du sens génésique. *Gazette médicale de Paris,* juillet 1849.

BROCA. Masturbation invétérée. Infibulation. *Bulletin de la Société de chirurgie de Paris,* t. V, s. 2, p. 10.

BROUARDEL. Étude critique sur la valeur des signes attribués à la pédérastie. *Annales d'hygiène publique,* 1880, n° 20, p. 182.

— Des empêchements au mariage et l'hermaphrodisme en particulier. Hermaphrodisme, impuissance, type infantile, saphisme, etc. *Gazette des Hôpitaux,* 1ᵉʳ et 18 janvier, 1ᵉʳ et 8 février 1887.

BUCHER, E. Lehrbuch der gerichtsärztlichen Medizin, 1872, II Aufl., p. 197.

BUFFON. Histoire naturelle de l'homme. Puberté.

BULTHAUPT, H. Narzissus. Roman, Vom Fels zum Meer. September, 1886.

BURTON, SIR R. F. Appendix and Anthropological Notes in "The Thousand Nights and a Night."

CANLER (Ancien chef de la sûreté). Mémoires. Brussels, 1862.

CANTARANO, G. Contribuzione alla casuistica della inversione dell' istinto sessuale. *La Psichiatria, la Neuropatologia e le scienze affini.* Naples, 1883.

— Inversione e pervertimenti dell' istinto sessuale. *La Psichiatria,* 1890, Fasc. 3 and 4.

CARLIER. Les deux prostitutions.

CARPENTER, EDWARD. De l'Amour homogénique et de sa place dans une société libre. *Société Nouvelle.*

CASA, JOANNE DELLA. In laudem Sodomitorum. Capitolo supra il forno. Opere. Venezia, 1752.

CASPER. Klinische Novellen zur gerichtlichen Medizin. Berlin, 1863.

— Ueber Nothzucht und Päderastie. *Vierteljahrsber. f. Gerichtl. Medizin,* 1852.

— Praktisches Handbuch der Gerichtlichen Medizin.

CATTELANI, GIORGIO. Il peccato supremo. "Turpi amori". Naples, 1893.

CHARCOT et MAGNAN. Inversion du sens génital. *Archives de Neurologie,* 1882.

— Inversion du sens génital et autres perversions sexuelles. *Annales médico-psychologiques.* 1ʳᵉ sér., tome 1. Paris, 1885.

CHEVALIER, JULIEN. De l'inversion de l'instinct sexuel au point de vue médico-légal. Paris, Octave Doin, 1885.

— De l'inversion sexuelle aux points de vue clinique, anthropologique et médico-légal. *Archives de l'anthropologie criminelle et des sciences pénales.* Paris-Lyon, tome 5, 1890; 6ᵉ tome, 1891.

COFFIGNON, CL. La corruption à Paris.

COELIUS AURELIANUS. Ueber "Parmenides oder über die Natur". Die Erblichkeit der griechischen Liebe. Bâle, 1529.

COHEN. Drei juristische Aufsätze. Berlin, 1893.

COHN, PROF. HERMAN. Augenkrankheiten bei Masturbanten. *Neurologisches Centralblatt,* 1883, p. 63.

CORNELIUS NEPOS. Vitae. Alcibiades.

COUTAGNE. Notes sur la Sodomie. *Lyon médical,* nᵒˢ 35, 36. 1880.

CRAMER. Die conträre Sexualempfindung in ihren Beziehungen zum § 175 des Strafgezetzbuches. *Klin. Wochenschrift,* 43 and 44, 1897.

CROTHERS, F. D. Inebriate Automatism, *The Journal of nervous and mental disease,* Vol. 2.

CULLERRE. Des perversions sexuelles chez les persécutés. *Annales médico-psychologiques.* Paris, mars 1886.

DALLEMAGNE, J. Dégénérés et déséquilibrés. Bruxelles-Paris, 1895.

DÉMEAUX. Priapisme spontané. *Annales de la Chirurgie française et étrangère,* 1841, vol. III, p. 403.

DEMME. Buch der Verbrechen.

DESCURET. La médecine des passions. Paris, 1860.

DESSOIR, MAX. Zur Psychologie der vita sexualis. *Zeitschrift für Psychologie,* vol. 50.

DIDEROT. La Religieuse.

DIEZ, E. A. Der Selbstmord, 1838.

DIGATIO. Eros, roman. Leipzig, Wilh. Friedrichs, 1898.

DIPHILUS. Päderastæ.

DOHRN, F. Zur Lehre von der Päderastie. *Caspers Vierteljahrsschrift.* 7 vol. 2 fasc. Berlin, 1855.

DOSTOYEVSKY. The House of the Dead.

DOUGLAS, LORD ALFRED. Poèmes, Paris, 1896.
Introduction à mes poèmes avec quelques considérations sur l'affaire Oscar Wilde. *Revue blanche,* juin 1896.

DUBARRY, ARMAND. Les invertis. Paris, 1896.

DUFOUR, PIERRE. Histoire de la prostitution chez tous les peuples du monde, etc., 8 vol., 1851-54.
— Mémoires curieux sur l'histoire des mœurs et de la prostitution en France aux XVII⁰ et XVIII⁰ siècles, 1854.

DUGAS, L. L'amitié antique d'après les mœurs populaires et les théories des philosophes. Paris, 1894.

DUMONT d'URVILLE. Voyages dans les mers du Sud. Paris, 1841-1845.

ELLIS, HAVELOCK. Sexual inversion with an analysis of thirty-three new cases. *Bulletin of the psychological section of the Medico-legal Society,* New York, December, 1895. Vol. III, n° IV.
— Studies in the Psychology of Sex. Philadelphia, 1901-1928.

ERASMUS, DESIDERIUS. Lesbos.

ERKELENS, WILHELM VAN. Strafgesetz und widernatürliche Unzucht. Berlin, 1895. Kornfeldsche Buchhandlung.

EUBULOS. Ganymedes.

EULENBURG, ALBERT. Sexuale Neuropathie. Leipzig, 1895.

— Aus der Art. Roman. Nord und Süd. 1883-1884.

— § 175. Aufsatz in der Wochenschrift *"Zunkunft"*. Jahrgang VI, n° 31, 1898.

EUPOLIS. Baptai.

EURIPIDES. Chrysippos.

FAHNER. System der gerichtl. Arzneikunde. Bd. III, p. 186.

FALRET. Sur les perversions génitales, *Annales médico-psychologiques,* 7ᵉ série, t. I, p. 472. Paris, 1885.

FÉRÉ, CHARLES. La descendance d'un inverti. *Revue générale de clinique et de thérapeutique,* 1896.

— Sexual Degeneration. New York, 1932. Anthropological Press.

FEYDEAU. La comtesse de Chalis. Paris, 1863.

FILIPPI, A. Manuele di aphrodisiologia civile, criminale e venere forense. Pisa, 1878.

FINK, H. P. Romantische Liebe und persönliche Schönheit. Deutsch von Udo Brachvogel. Breslau, 1890.

FLAUBERT, GUSTAVE. Salammbô.

FORBERG. See Beccadelli.

FORSTER, J. R. Justizmorde im 19 Jahrhundert. Ein Notschrei an das Volk. Zürich, 1898. Selbstverlag des Verfassers.

FRÄNKEL. Der Geisteszustand der Päder-
asten, 1869.

— "Homo mollis". *Mediz. Zeitung des
Vereins für Heilkunde in Preus-
sen.* 28ᵉ vol. 1853.

FRANZ, ADOLPH. Ein Fall von Paranoia
mit Konträrer Sexualempfindung. Doktordiss.
Berlin, 1895.

FREDERIKSEN. Adriano.

FRENTZEL. De Sodomia. Erfurt, 1723.

FREY, LUDWIG. Der Eros und die Kunst.
Ethische Studien. Leipzig, 1896,
Max Spohr.

— Die Männer des Rätsels und der §
175 des deutschen Reichsstrafgesetzbuches. Leipzig, 1898. Max
Spohr.

FRIEDREICH, J. B. Handbuch der gerichtsärztlichen Praxis, 1843. Bd. I, p. 271.

GARNIER. Les fétichistes, pervertis et invertis sexuels. Paris, 1896.

— Onanisme seul et à deux sous toutes
ses formes. Paris, 1884.

GAZETTE DES HÔPITAUX, 1852, p. 10.
Érections génitales morbides chez l'homme.

GEIGEL. Geschichte und Therapie der Syphilis.

GESNER, JOH. MATTH. Socrates sanctus
Paederasta. Trajecti ad Rhenum, 1769.

GIRALDÈS et HORTELOUP. Sur un cas
de meurtre avec viol sodomique, *Annales
d'hygiène publique,* 1874, p. 419.

GLEY, E. Les aberrations de l'instinct sexuel.
Revue philosophique, 1884.

GOCK, VON. Beitrag zur Kenntniss der conträren Sexualempfindung, *Arch. für Psych.,* Bd. V, p. 564, 1875.

GOETHE, JOH. WOLFG. von. Elégie sur un jeune Romain.

GRABOWSKY, NORBERT. Die verkehrte Geschlechtsempfindung oder die mannmännliche und weibweibliche Liebe. Leipzig, 1894, Max Spohr.

— Die mannweibliche Natur des Menschen mit Berücksichtigung des psychosexuellen Hermaphroditismus. Leipzig, 1897, Max Spohr.

GREVERUS, J. P. Zur Würdigung, Erklärung und Kritik der Idyllen Theokrits. Oldenburg, 1845.

GRIESINGER. Ueber einen wenig bekannten psychopatischen Zustand. *Arch. für Psych.,* I, p. 651. Berlin, 1868.

GRILL. Die Lehre von der Psychopathia sexualis und ihre gerichtsärztliche Bedeutung. *Ugeskrift for Läger,* 4 R. XXVIII, n°s 27, 33.

GRILLPARZER. Selbstbiographie, Tagebücher.

GROHE, MELCHIOR. Der Urning vor Gericht. Ein forensischer Dialog. Leipzig, Max Spohr.

GROSS. Geschlechtliche Verirrungen. *Encyclopädie des Erziehungs und Unterrichtswesens.* 1878.

GUTTZEIT, JOHANNES. Naturrecht oder Verbrechen? Eine Studie über weibliche Liebe bei Männern und umgekehrt. Verlag Wilh. Besser, Leipzig.

GUYOT, YVES. La prostitution. Paris, 1883.

GYSBRECHTS. Observation de priapisme, *Journal de Médecine de Bruxelles,* 1848, vol. VII, p. 223.

HAFIZ. Poems.

HAGEN, KARL von. Die Geschlechtsbestimmung des werdenden Menschen. Berlin, H. Steinitz, 1898. Worin besteht die Ursache des Geschlechtsdrangs? Dresden, 1898.

HAHN, JOH. GEORG von. Albanesische Studien, 1854.

HALM, M. Die Liebe des Uebermenschen. Ein neues Lebensgesetz. Leipzig, Max Spohr.

HAMILTON, ALLAN McLANE. The civil responsibility of sexual perverts. *American Journal of Insanity,* April, 1896, n° 4.

HAMMOND. Sexual Impotence in the Male. New York, 1883.

HANDL. Der Wilde-Prozess. *Zeit* von Bahr. Wien, 15 Juni 1895, n° 37.

HARTMANN. Pædicatorem noxium esse. Frankfurt, 1776.

HARTMANN, O. O. Das Problem der Homosexualität im Lichte der Schopenhauerschen Philosophie. Leipzig, Max Spohr.

HARTUNG V. HARTUNGEN, M. U. Ueber virile Schwäche, etc. Wien, 1884, p. 188.

HATTÉ. Sur le Satyriasis ou Saturiasme. *Recueil périodique de médecine, chir. et pharmacie,* 1755, t. II, p. 109.

HEINSE. Italien's Liebesleben. Berlin, 1869.
— Begebenheiten des Encolp. Bonn, 1770.

HENNE AM RHYN, OTTO. Kulturgeschichte der Neuzeit. I Auflage. Leipzig, 1870.

HERMANN, HANS. Die Schuld der Väter, oder: Ist die gleichgeschlechtliche Liebe eine Sünde? Roman. Leipzig, Max Spohr.

HERMANT, ABEL. La mission de J.-B. Cruchod, roman.

— 2ᵉ édition sous le titre "Le Disciple aimé". Paris, Ollendorff, 1895.

HEYSE, PAUL. Hadrian.

HIRSCHFELD, M. § 175 des Reichs-Strafgesetz-Buches. Die homosexuelle Frage im Urteil der Zeitgenossen. Leipzig, 1898, Max Spohr.

— Der urnische Mensch. Leipzig, 1903.

— Berlins Dritte Geschlecht. Berlin, 1904.

— Die Homosexualität. Berlin, 1914.

HOCHE, CL. Zur Frage der forensischen Beurteilung sexueller Vergehen. *Neurolog. Centralblatt*. Leipzig, 1896.

HÖCK. Kreta.

HOFMANN, C. Päderastie. *Real-Encyclopädie der gesammten Heilkunde*. Vol. X, p. 294. 1882.

HOFMANN, EDUARD von. Lehrbuch der gerichtl. Medizin. 7 Aufl. Wien u. Leipzig, 1885, p. 52 and 104.

HÖGEL, HUGO. Die Verkehrtheit des Geschlechtstriebes im Strafrechte. *Gerichtssaal*, 53 vol., 1 and 2 fasc. Stuttgart, 1836.

HÖLDERLIN. Hyperion.

HOLLÄNDER, ALEX. Ein Beitrag zur Lehre von der Konträren Sexualempfindung. *Allgem. Wiener medizin. Zeitung*, nᵒˢ 37, 38, 40. 1882.

HOLTER, KARL von. Schwarzwaldau. Prague and Leipzig, 1856.

HÖSSLI, HEINRICH. Der Eros der Griechen oder Forschungen über Platonische Liebe. Ueber die Unzulässigkeit der äusseren Kennzeichen im Geschlechtsleben des Leibes und der Seele. Glarus, 1836. Saint-Gall, 1838.

HUBERT, M. L'inversion génitale et la législation. Bruxelles, 1892.

HÜPEDEN. Bemerkungen zu v. Krafft-Ebings "Der Konträrsexuale vor dem Strafrichter". *Gerichtssaal,* vol. 51, fasc. 5 and 6. Stuttgart, 1895.

HUTTEN, KARL von. Die Knabenliebschaften des Jesuiten-paters Marell. Leipzig, 1890.

JACKSON, CHARLES. L'amour sélectif. *Revue Blanche,* 1ᵉʳ octobre 1896.

JACOB, BIBLIOPHILE. Curiosités de l'Histoire de France. Causes célèbres, Paris, 1859.

JACOBS, FR. Vermischte Schriften. II, p. 212-254.

JACOBUS X***, DR. Genital Laws, their Observance and Violation.
— Untrodden Fields of Anthropology, Observations on the Esoteric Manners and Customs of semi-civilised Peoples. Paris, Carrington, 1895.
— A Medico-Legal Examination of the Abuses, Aberrations and Crimes of the Genital sense.
— The Ethnology of the Sixth Sense, its Anomalies, Perversions and Follies.
— The Basis of Passional Psychology.

JAGER, GUSTAV. Entdeckung der Seele. Stuttgart, 1884.

JAHRBUCH FÜR SEXUELLE ZWISCH-ENSTUFEN. (Annual for Sexual Intermediate Stages.) Magnus Hirschfeld, editor.

JEANNEL DE BORDEAUX. De la prostitution publique, et parallèle complet de la prostitution romaine et de la prostitution contemporaine. Paris, 1863. 2ᵉ éd.

JODELLE, ETIENNE. Le triomphe de Sodome. *Œuvres et mélanges poétiques.*

JOUX, OTTO de. [Ps. of Otto Rudolf Podjukl.] Die Enterbten des Liebesglückes oder das dritte Geschlecht. Ein Beitrag zur Seelenkunde. Leipzig, Max Spohr.
— Die hellenische Liebe in der Gegenwart. Psychologische Studien. Leipzig, 1897, Max Spohr.

JUSTI, CARL. J. J. Winckelmann, sein Leben, seine Werke, und seine Zeitgenossen. Leipzig, 1886.

JUVENAL. Satires.

KAAN. Psychopathia sexualis. Leipzig, 1844.

KELP. Ueber den Geisteszustand der Ehefrau C. M. *Allgemeine.*

KIERNAN, JOS. G. Responsibility in sexual perversion, *American Journal of Neur. and Psych.* 1882.
— Psychological aspects of the sexual appetite, *Alienist and Neurogolist.* Saint Louis, 1891.

KIRN, DR. L. Ueber die klinische forensische Bedeutung des perversen sexualtriebes. *Allg. Zeitschr. f. Psych.* Vol. XXXIX, p. 216.

KITIS, JOSEF. Die neuen Hellenen. Gedicht aus "Lyrische Radierungen". Wien, Leipzig, 1898.

KLINGER, FRIEDS. MAX von. Fausts Leben, Thaten und Höllenfahrt. Petersburg, 1791.

KLOPFER, KARL. Zwei Dichter, roman.

KLOSE. Ueber Päderastie in gerichtlich-medizinischer Hinsicht, in *Ersch und Gruber's Allgem. Encyclopädie.* 3 Sect. 9. Theil. Leipzig, 1837.

KOWALEWSKI, P. J. Die Primäre Verrücktheit. Für Aerzte und Juristen verfasst. 1881.

— Forensisch-psychiatrische Analysen. 2 Theile; für Aerzte und Juristen. 1881.

KOWALEWSKY, L. S. Ueber Perversion des Geschlechtssinnes bei Epileptischen. *Jahrb. für Psych.* 7 B. 3 Fasc. Leipzig u. Wien, 1887.

KRAEPELIN, ÉMILE. Psychiatrie. 4. Aufl. Leipzig, 1893.

KRAFFT-EBING. Der Konträrsexuale vor dem Strafrichter. Leipzig u. Wien, 1894. Franz Deuticke, ed.

— Konträre Sexualempfindung vom klinisch-forensischen Standpunkt. *Allge. Zeitschrift für Psych.* V, 38, 1838.

— Psychopathia sexualis mit besonderer Berücksichtigung der konträren Sexualempfindung. Eine klinisch-forensische Studie. 10 Aufl. Stuttgart, 1898. Ferd. Encke, Ed.

— Ueber gewisse Anomalien des Geschlechtstriebes, etc. *Arch. Psych. u. Nervenkr.* 1877, VII, p. 291.

— Zur Lehre von der konträren Sexualempfindung. *Irrenfreund.* 1884. Nº 1.

— Zur Erklärung der konträren Sexualempfindung. *Jahrb. für Psychiatrie und Nervenheilkunde.* V. 13.
Fasc. I.

KRATINOS. Malttrakoi.

KRAUSS, A. Die Psychologie des Verbrechens. Tubingen. 1884, p. 173.

KRIESE. Beitrag zur Lehre von der conträren
Sexualempfindung in ihrer klinisch-forensis-
chen Bedeutung. (Inaugural-Dissertation.)
Würzburg, 1898.

KRUEG, JULIUS. Perverted sexual instincts. *Brain,* vol. IV. London, 1882.

KUPFFER, ELISAR von. Ehrlos (Ver-
lobt). Eckstein, 1898.

KURELLA. Die Theorie der Konträren Sexualempfindung. *Zentralbl. für
Nervenheilkunde und Psychiatrie,*
19 Jahrg. Febr. 1896.

— Zum biologischen Verständnis der so-
matischen und psychischen Bisex-
ualität. *Zentralbl. für Nervenheilkunde und Psych.* 15 Jahrg. Mai
1896.

LACASSAGNE, PROF. Article "Pédérastie" dans le *Dict. encyclop. des
sciences médicales.*

— Attentats à la pudeur. *Arch. d'an-
throp. criminelle,* 1896. Vol. I.

LAKER. Ueber eine besondere Form von
Perversion des weiblichen Geschlechtstriebes.
Archiv. für Gynäkologie, 34ᵉ vol.

LANGNER, NORBERT. Echte Liebe.
Skizze aus dem Leben in *"der Eigene".* II
Jahrg. Fasc. I. 1898.

LASÈGUE, BROUARDEL et MOTET. Rapport sur l'affaire Menesclou, *Annales d'hygiène publique*. 1880, p. 439.

LASÈGUE. Les Exhibitionnistes, *Union Médicale*. 1877, 1er mai.

LAUPTS, DR. Perversion et perversité sexuelles. Préface par Emile Zola. Paris, 1896.

LAURENT, ÉMILE. Les bisexués gynécomastes et hermaphrodites. Paris, 1894.
— Sadisme et Masochisme. Paris, Vigot, 1903.

LEGLUDIC, H. Attentats aux mœurs. Notes et observations de médecine légale. Paris, 1896.

LEGRAIN. Des anomalies de l'instinct sexuel et en particulier du sens génital. Paris, 1896.

LEGRAND DU SAULLE. La Folie devant les tribunaux.
— Les signes physiques des folies raisonnantes, *Annales médico-psychologiques*, Mai 1876.

LENHOSSEK, MICHAEL von. Darstellung des menschlichen Gemüts. Wien, 1834.

LENORMANT, C. Quæstio cur Plato Aristophanem in convivium introduxerit. Paris, 1838.

LEONARDSON, PETR. GUST. Mythicum de amore et animo philophemæ Platonis Phædro. Upsala, 1830.

LEONPACHER. Psychische Impotenz. Konträre Geschlechtsempfindung. *Friedreichs Blätter für gerichtliche Medizin und Sanitätspolizei*. 18 Jahrgang. Nürnberg, 1887.

LIESEGANG, RAPH. ED. "Das bist du".
Leipzig, 1896, Max Spohr.

LINKE. "Endymion"—Hadrian und Antinous.—Zwei epische Gedichte. Münden i. W.
von J. C. C. Bruns.

LOMBARD, JEAN. L'Agonie.—Byzance.

LOMBROSO, CESARE. Amore nei pazzi.
Amore invertito. *Archivio d. Psich.* 1881.
— Verzeni e Agnoletti. Rome, 1874.
— Amori anomali e precoci nei pazzi *Arch. di. Psich.,* etc. 1883, VI.
— Le neurosi in Dante e Michelangelo, *Archivio di psichiatria, scienze penali e antropologia criminale.* Florence, Turin, Rome, 1894.

LOMBROSO, C. et G. FERRERO. La donna delinquente, la prostituta e la donna normale. Turin, Rome, 1894.

LUDWIG, J. Der § 175 des Reichsstrafgesetzbuches Streitfragen. *Wissenschaftl. Fachorgan der deutschen Sittlichkeitsvereine.* 1 Fasc. Berlin, 1892.

LUIZ. Les fellatores. Paris.

LUZENBERGER, AUGUSTO DI. Sul mecanismo dei pervertimenti sessuali e loro terapia. *Archivio di psichop. sess.* Rome, Naples, 1-15 Oct. 1895. Vol. I.

MADJEWSKI, JULIAN. Pamiatki.

MAGNAN. Des anomalies, des aberrations et des perversions sexuelles. Paris, 1885.

MAIZEROY, RENÉ. Les deux Amies.

MANTEGAZZA. The Sexual Relations of Mankind. New York, 1932.

MARLOWE, CHR. Edward the Second.

MARTIAL. Epigrams.

MARTINEAU, L. Leçons sur les déformations vulvaires et anales. Paris, 1884.

MARX, HEINRICH. Urningsliebe. Die sittliche Hebung Urningtums und die Streichung des § 175 des deutschen Strafgesetzbuches. Leipzig, 1875.

MASCHKA, S. Unzucht wider Natur, *Handbuch der gerichtl. Med.* 1882. Vol. III, p. 176.

— *Prager med. Viertelj.* Vol. 89.

MASIUS. Handbuch der gerichtl. Arzneiwissenschaft. I, p. 264. 1831.

MASSIMI, PACIFICO. Hecatelegium ou les cent élégies satiriques et gaillardes de Pacifico Massimi, poète d'Ascoli (XVᵉ siècle), litéralement traduit pour la première fois, texte latin en regard. Paris, Liseux, 1885.

MAUPASSANT, GUY DE. La femme de Paul, nouvelle.

MEDICAL TIMES & GAZETTE (1852). Sᵗ Bartholomew's Hospital; obstinate priapism.

MEIBOMIUS, J. H. De Flagrorum usu in re venerea. London, 1770.

MEIER, C. Ueber Päderastie im Alterthum in *Ersch und Gruber's Allg. Encyclopädie.* 3. Sect. 9. Theil. Leipzig, 1837.

MEINERS. Ueber die Männerliebe der Griechen, nebst einem Auszuge aus dem Gastmahl des Platon. *Verm. philos. Schriften.* 1 Theil.

MENDE. Handbuch der gerichtl. Medizin. Leipzig, 1826. Vol. IV, p. 506.

MENDÈS. Méphistophela.

— La maison de la vieille.

— Zo-har.

MENIÈRE, P. Études médicales sur les Poètes latins. Paris, 1858. V. Juvénal, p. 351, et Martial, p. 433.

MÉRY. Monsieur Auguste. Paris, 1860.

MEYHOFER. Zur konträren Sexualempfindung. *Zeitschrift für Medizinalbeamte.* 5 Jahrg. N° 16. Aug. 1892.

MICHEA. Des déviations maladives de l'appétit vénérien. *Union médicale.* Paris, 1846.

MICHEL. Histoire des races maudites de la France et de l'Espagne. Paris, 1847. (Les Cagots.)

MIERZEJEWSKI, W. Legal Gynecology. Saint-Petersburg, 1878. (In Russian.)

MIRBEAU, OCTAVE. Sébastien Roch, roman. Paris, Charpentier.

MOLL, ALBERT. Die konträre Sexualempfindung. Berlin, 1893. Fischers medizin. Buchhandlung.
— Untersuchungen über die Libido sexualis. Berlin, 1897.

MONIN, E. Misères nerveuses. Paris, 1890.

MONTAGNE, E. Histoire de la prostitution dans l'antiquité.

MORAUD. Collection de plusieurs observations singulières sur des corps étrangers appliqués aux parties naturelles, *Mém. de l'Acad. royale chir.*, 1757.

MOREAU DE TOURS, DR. Des aberrations du sens génésique. Paris, 1880.

NEGRI, CAVAL. de. Januskopf.

NEGRIS. De la dynamie ou exaltation fonctionnelle au début de la paralysie générale. Paris, 1878.

NERI, S. A. Pervertito, necrofiliaco, peder-
asta, masochista. *Archivio delle psicopatie sessuali.* Vol. I, fasc. 7. Rome, Naples, Apr. 1898.

OLD MAN YOUNG AGAIN, THE. Oth-
erwise entitled in Arabic the book of The Re-
turn of the Old Man to the Condition of the
Strength of Youthtide in the Power of Coition.
Literally translated from the Arabic by AN
ENGLISH "BOHEMIAN". *Kitab "Ruju'a as-
Shaykh ila Sabah fi-'l-Kuwwat 'ala-l Bah"*
With Translator's Foreword; On the Age and
Authorship of the Book; On the Various Kinds
of Impotence, with a Description of the Degrees of Virility and the Power of Erection;
The Romance of the Genital Instinct; Aphrodisiacs, their History, Nature and Use; Nu-
merous important Notes Illustrating the Text,
and an Excursus.

PALLAVICINI, FERRANTE. Alcibiade
fanciullo a Scuola, 1652.

PANIZZA, OSK. Bayreuth und die Homo-
　　　　　　　sexualität. Gesellschaft von Con-
　　　　　　　rad. XI Jahrg. Fasc. I, 1895.
　—　　Das Liebeskonzil, Tragiekomödie.
　　　　　　　Zurich. Schabeltitz.

PARENT - DUCHÂTELET. La prostitution dans la ville de Paris, 1857. Tome I, p.
214.

PAW, M. de. Philosophische Untersuchungen.

PENTA, P. Caratteri generali, origine e sig-
nificato dei pervertimenti sessuali, dimostrati
colle autobiografie di Alfieri e di Rousseau e
col dialogo "gli amore" di Luciano. *Archivio delle psicopatie sessuali.* Vol. I. Fasc. I.
Rome, Naples, 1890.

PENTA, P. e A. d'URSO. Sopra un caso d'inversione sessuale in una donna epileptica. *Arch. delle psicop. sess.* Vol. I. Fasc. III. Feb. 1896.

PETRONIUS. Satyricon.

PEYER, ALEXANDER. Ein Beitrag zur Lehre von der konträren Sexualempfindung. *Münch. med. Wochenschrift.* 10 Juni 1890. N° 23.

PITAVAL. Causes célèbres. Tome VIII, p. 511.

PLATEN, GRAF AUGUST. Poèmes.
— Tagebücher. Herausgegeben von G. V. Laubmann und L. von Scheffler. Stuttgart, 1898.

PLATO. The Symposium.
— Phaedrus.
— Lysis.

PLEHN. Lesbiacorum liber. Berlin, 1896.

PLUTARCH. Erotes. Einleitung zum Commentar. v. A. W. Winkelmann.

POUILLET, DR. De l'onanisme chez l'homme. Paris, 1897.

PRAXILLA. Zeus and Chrysippos.

RABOW. Ueber angeborene konträre Sexualempfindung. *Zeitschrift für klin. Medizin.* 17e vol. Supplement. Berlin, 1890.
— Zur Casuistik der angeborenen conträren Sexualempfindung. *Centralblatt f. Nervenheilk. u. Psych.,* 1883, p. 186.

RABUTAUX, A. De la prostitution en Europe depuis l'antiquité jusqu'à la fin du XVIe siécle. 1865.

RACHILDE. Monsieur Vénus. Préface de
Maurice Barrès.
— Les Hors-Nature.
— Madame Adonis.

RAFFALOVICH, MARC - ANDRE.
Uranisme et unisexualité.
— Die Entwicklung der Homosexualität.
— Referat über John Addington Symonds, H. F. Brown, London,
1894.

RAGGI. Aberrazione del sentimento sessuale
in un maniaco ginecomasta. *La Salute,* 1882.
N° 11, p. 86.

**RAMDOHR, FRIEDRICH WILHELM
BERNH.** von. Venus Urania. Leipzig,
1798.

RAMIEN, TH. Sappho und Socrates, oder
Wie erklärt sich die Liebe der Männer und
Frauen zu Personen des eigenen Geschlechtes?
Leipzig, 1896. Max Spohr.

REBELL, HUGUES. Défense d'Oscar
Wilde. *Mercure de France.* Paris,
1895.
— La Nichina, roman.

REICH. Ueber Unsittlichkeit. Berlin, 1866.

REUSS. Des aberrations du sens génésique
chez l'homme. *Annales d'hygiène publique et
de médecine légale,* III° série. Paris, 1886.

REY, J. L. Des prostituées et de la prostitution
en général, 1847.

RITTI. De l'attraction des sexes semblables.
Gaz. hebdom. de méd. et de chir. 4 janvier
1878.

RODE, LEON de. L'inversion génitale et la
législation. Bruxelles, 1892.

ROMER, A. Das Sittengesetz vor dem Richterstuhl einer ärztlichen Autorität. Streitfragen. *Wissenschaftl. Fachorgan der deutschen Sittlichkeitsvereine.* Berlin, 1892.

ROSENBAUM, DR. JULIUS. Geschichte der Lustseuche im Alterthum, nebst ausführlichen Untersuchungen über den Venus und Phalluscultus, Bordelle, Νουσος θήλεα der Skythen, Pæderastie und andere geschlechtliche Ausschweifungen der Alten, als Beiträge zur richtigen Erklärung ihrer Schriften. Halle a. S. 1893.

The Plague of Lust in classical antiquity, including detailed investigations into the cult of Venus and Phallic Worship, Brothels, the Νουσος Θήλεα (Feminine disease) of the Scythians, Pæderastia, and other sexual perversions amongst the Ancients, as contributions towards the exact interpretation of their writings. Paris, 1902.

ROUBAUD. Traité de l'impuissance et de la stérilité. Paris, 1876.

ROUSSEAU, J. J. Confessions, part I, book I.

RUL-OGER. Priapisme et pollutions nocturnes. *Journ. de méd. de Bruxelles,* 1848. Vol. VI, p. 19.

SAADI. Gulistan.

SACHER-MASOCH, LEOP. von. Die Liebe des Plato.
— Venus in Furs.

SAURY. Étude clinique sur la folie héréditaire, 1886.

SAVAGE, GEORGE H. Case of a sexual perversion in a man. *The Journal of Mental Science,* vol. XXX, October 1884.

SCHOERING, DR. La prostitution en Chine.

SHAW, J. C. and FERRIS, S. N. Perverted sexual instinct. *The Journal of Nervous and Mental Disease,* 1883. N° 2.

SCHAUKAHL, RICHARD. Verse. Brünn, 1896, Rudolf Rohrers Verlag.

SCHILLER, FRIEDR. von. Spiel des Schicksals.

— Entwurf zum Drama: "Die Malteser". Crequi und St-Priest.

SCHMINKE. Ein Fall von conträrer Sexualempfindung. *Arch. f. psychol.* Vol. III, 1872, p. 225.

SCHOLZ. Bekenntnisse eines an perverser Geschlechtsrichtung Leidenden. *Vierteljahresschr. f. gerichtl. Med.,* 1873.

SCHOPENHAUER, A. Die Welt als Wille und Vorstellung, 1859. Vol. II, p. 641.

— Metaphysik der Geschlechtsliebe.

SCHRENCK-NOTZING. Beiträge zur forensischen Beurteilung von Sittlichkeitsvergehen mit besonderer Berücksichtigung der Pathogenese psycho-sexueller Anomalien. *Archiv. für Kriminal-Anthropologie und Kriminalistik.* Bd. I.

— Die Suggestiontherapie bei krankhaften Erscheinungen d. Geschlechtssinnes, 1892.

— Ein Beitrag zur Aetiologie der konträren Sexualempfindung. Wien, 1895.

— Literaturzusammenstellung über die Psychologie und Psychopathologie der vita sexualis. *Zeitschrift für Hypnose,* VII, 1, 2; VIII, 2.

SCHURING. De coitu nefando seu Sodomia. Gynäkologie. Sect. II, cap. VII.

SEIFFERT (Just. Ad. Joh). Kosmogonie. Potsdam, 1881.

SÉRIEUX, PAUL. Recherches cliniques sur les anomalies de l'instinct sexuel. Paris, 1898.

SERO, OS. Der Fall Wilde und das Problem der Homosexualität. Ein Prozess und ein Interview. Leipzig, 1896, Max Spohr.

SERVAES. Zur Kenntniss von der conträren Sexualempfindung. *Arch. f. Psych.*, 1876. Vol. VI, p. 484.

SEYDEL, C. Die Beurteilung des perversen Sexualvergehen in foro. *Vierteljahrschrift f. gerichtl. Med. u, öffentl. Sanitätswesen.* Dritte Folge, 5 vol. Berlin, 1893.

SHAKESPEARE, WILLIAM. Sonnets.

SHAW, J. C. and FERRIS, S. N. On perverted sexual instincts. *The Journal of Nervous and Mental Disease.* N° 2, 1883.

SIEMERLING, E. Kasuistische Beiträge zur forensischen Psychiatrie. *Neurol. Zentralblatt,* 1896.

SNOO, de. Fall von angeborener conträrer Sexualempfindung. *Psychiatr. Bladen.* XII, 2-4; XIII, 3.

SOUILLAC, MAURICE de. Zé 'boïm roman saphique. Paris, Brossier.

SPRENGEL. Geschichte der Medicin. 2. Aufl., p. 83.

STADION, EMERICH GRAF. Drei seltsame Erinnerungen. Bochnia, W. Pisz, 1868.

STALLBAUM. Diatribe in Mythum Platonis de divino amoris ortu. Leipzig, 1854.

STARK. Ueber conträre Sexualempfindung. *Allgem. Zeitschr f. Psychol.*, 1877. Vol. XXXIX, p. 209.

STEGLEHNER, GEORG. De hermaphroditorum natura tractatus anatomico-physiologico-pathologicus. Bamberg & Leipzig, 1817.

STERZ, DR. Beiträge zur Lehre von der conträren Sexualempfindung. *Jahrb. f. Psych.* Vol. III. Heft 3, p. 221.

STOLTENBERG. Diss. in pædicatorem noxium et infestum rei publicæ civem. 1775.

SUETONIUS. History of the Twelve Caesars.

SUIDAS. Pædica.

SULLIVAN, WILLIAM C. Notes on a case of acute insanity with sexual perversion. *The Journal of Mental Science.* April, 1893.

SYMONDS, JOHN ADDINGTON.
A Problem in Greek Ethics.
— A Problem in Modern Ethics.

TALBOT, E. S. A case of developmental degenerative insanity, with sexual inversion, melancholia, following removal of testicles, attempted murder and suicide. *The Journal of Mental Science.* April, 1896.

TAMASSIA. Sull' inversione dell' instinto sessuale. *Rivista sperini di frenitria e di medicina legale.* 1878. T. XV, p. 97.

TARDI. L'Amour morbide.

TARDIEU. Étude médico-légale sur les attentats aux mœurs. 7e éd. 1878.

TAXIL, LÉO. La Prostitution contemporaine, 1884.

TAYLOR. Medical Jurisprudence. 1873, II, p. 473.

THAL, WILHELM. Der Roman eines Konträr-Sexuellen: mit einer Einleitung: "Der Uranismus" von Raffalovich. Leipzig, 1899, Max Spohr.

THEOCRITUS. Idyls.

THOINOT, L. Attentats aux mœurs et perversion du sens génital. Paris, 1898.

TIBULLUS. Elegies.

TORGGLER. Kasuistischer Beitrag zur Perversion des weiblichen Geschlechtstriebes. *Wiener Klinische Wochenschrift*, 1889, n° 28.

TOULMOUCHE. Des attentats à la pudeur et du viol. *Annales d'hygiène publique*, 1868.

TOVOTE, HEINZ. Heisses Blut. Erlöst.

TRITHENICIUS, JOHANNES. Opera historica. 2 Bde. 1601. Frankfurt a. M. Bemerkung über Faust.

TYBALT, LAURENT TAILHADE. Chronique sur l'affaire Oscar Wilde. *Écho de Paris*, 29 mai 1895.

ULRICH, A. von. Homosexualität. *"Kritik,"* 18 januar 1898.

ULRICHS, KARL HEINRICH. Numa Numantius. Vindex social-juristiche Studien über mannmännliche Geschlechtsliebe. Leipzig, 1864.

— Inclusa. Anthropologische Studien über mannmännliche Geschlechtsliebe. Leipzig, 1864.

— Vindicta. Kampf für Freiheit von Verfolgung. Leipzig, 1865.

— Formatrix. Anthropologische Studien über urnische Liebe. Leipzig, 1865.

Ara Spei. Moralphilosophische und social philosophische Studien über urnische Liebe. Leipzig, 1865.

Gladius furens. Das Naturrätsel der Urningsliebe und der Irrtum der Gesetzgeber. Kassel, 1868.

Memnon I et II. Die Geschlechtsnatur des mannliebenden Urnings. Schleiz, 1867.

Incubus. Urningsliebe und Blutgier. Leipzig, 1869.

Argonauticus. Zastrow und die Urninge des pietistischen, ultramontanen und freidenkenden Lagers. Leipzig, 1869.

Prometheus. Beiträge zur Erforschung des Naturrätsels des Uranismus. Leipzig, 1870.

Araxes. Ruf nach Befreiung der Urningsnatur vom Strafgesetz. Schleiz, 1870.

Kritische Pfeile. Denkschrift über die Bestrafung der Urningsliebe. Leipzig, 1880.

§ 143 des preussischen Strafgesetzbuches. Leipzig, 1869.

Das Gemeinschädliche des § 143 des preuss. Strafgesetzbuches vom 14 April 1851 und seine notwendige Tilgung als § 152 im Entwurfe eines Strafgesestzbuches für den norddeutschen Bund. In Folge öffentlicher Aufforderung durch die Kommission des Strafgesetzbuches für den norddeutschen Bund.

230

— Auf Bienches Flügeln. Ein Flug um den Erdball in Epigrammen und poetischen Bildern. Leipzig, 1875 (2, 87, 96, 110, 111, 118, 137, 185, 187, 230, 231, 277).

— Matrosengeschichten. Leipzig, 1885.

URQUHART. Case of sexual perversion. *The Journal of Mental Science,* vol. XXXVII. January, 1891.

— Anastasius; Fahrten eines Griechen im Orient.

VACANO, EMIL MARIA. Humbug König Phantasus.

VAY, ADELMA FREIIN von. Studie über die Geisterwelt. II Aufl. Leipzig, 1874.

VELHUYSIUS, LAMBERTUS. Tractatus moralis de pudore et dignitate naturali hominis. P. 197.

VENTURI, SILVIO. Le degenerationi psico-sessuali. Turin, 1892.

VERLAINE, PAUL. Parallèlement.

— Paul Husson, nouvelle. *Revue indépendante,* 1888.

— Les mémoires d'un veuf.

VIAZZI, PIO. Sui reati sessuali. Note ed appunti di psicologia e giurisprudenza con prefazione del Prof. Enrico Morselli. Turin, 1896.

VIDAL et LEGRAND DU SAULLE. Annales médico-psychol., Vᵉ série, 1876. T. XV, p. 446.

VIGNALE, ANTONIO. La Cazzaria, dialogue priapique de l'Arsiccio Intronato, littéralement traduit pour la première fois, texte italien en regard. Paris-Liseux, 1882.

VILLIOT, JEAN de. Étude sur la Flagellation au point de vue médical, historique et religieux, un vol. in-8°. Carrington, éditeur.

VIREY. Histoire naturelle du genre humain. Paris, 1824.

VIRMAITRE, CHARLES. Mesdemoiselles Saturne.

— Flagellants et Flagellés de Paris. Carrington, éditeur.

WALTER, PROF. On Sexual Excitation and Coitus. *Ssowremennaja medicina.* 1862, p. 916, et 1863, p. 168. (In Russian.)

WEISBRODT, E. Die Sittlichkeitsverbrechen vor dem Gesetze. Historisch und kritisch beleuchtet. Berlin et Leipzig, A. H. Fried. & Co., 1891.

WEISSE, CHRISTIAN FÉLIX. Die Freunde. Trauerspiel.

WESTPHAL. *Arch. f. Psych. u. Nervenk.* 1869, p. 273.

— Die conträre Sexualempfindung. *Arch. f. Psych.,* 1870, II, p. 73.

— Zur conträren Sexualempfindung. *Arch. f. Psych.,* 1873, III, p. 225.

WIEGAND, WILH. Die wissenschaftliche Bedeutung der platonischen Liebe. Berlin, 1877.

WILBRANDT, ADOLF. Fridolins heimliche Ehe. 2 Auflage. Vienna, 1883. Dramatisiert als "Reise nach River."

WILDE, OSCAR. Dorian Grey.

WILPERT, JAMES von. Das Recht des dritten Geschlechts. Leipzig, 1898, Max Spohr.

WINCKELMANN, J. J. Abhandlungen über die Schönheit. *Wojenno-Medicinski Journal,* 1849. N° IV, p. 4. On pathologic perversion of the sex instinct. (In Russian.)

WOLFART, JOH. HEINR. Tractatio juridica de sodomia vera et spuria Hermaphroditi. 2° éd. Frankf. a. M. 1742.

ZACCHIAS, PAULUS. Quæstiones medico-legales. Līv. IV. T. II. Lugduni, 1726.

ZSCHOKKE, HEINRICH. Eros. Ein Gespräch über die Liebe. 1821.

ZUCCARELLI, ANGELO. Inversione congenita dell' istinto sessuale in due donne. Naples, 1888.

CPSIA information can be obtained at www.ICGtesting.com
Printed in the USA
LVOW08s1145060115

421707LV00001B/19/P